Contents

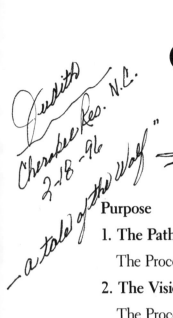

Handwritten notes: "Judith Cherokee Res. N.C. 2-18-96", "— a tale of the Wolf "

RAINBOW MEDICINE

A Visionary Guide to Native American Shamanism

WOLF MOONDANCE

Illustrated by Jim Sharpe & Sky Starhawk

Sterling Publishing Co., Inc. New York

To my family, spirit and blood.

✻ ✻ ✻ ✻ ✻ ✻ ✻ ✻

To our next generation

✻ ✻ ✻ ✻ ✻ ✻ ✻ ✻

And their generations to come.

To Raven and Hawk, all my love.

Library of Congress Cataloging-in-Publication Data

Moondance, Wolf.
    Rainbow medicine : a visionary guide to Native American shamanism /
Wolf Moondance ; illustrated by Jim Sharpe & Sky Starhawk.
       p.   cm.
    Includes index.
    ISBN 0-8069-0364-3
    1. Shamanism—United States—Miscellanea. 2. Indians of North
America—Religion and mythology—Miscellanea. I. Title.
BF1622.U6M66   1994
    299'.7—dc20   93-39600
                                                   CIP

10 9 8 7 6 5 4

Published 1994 by Sterling Publishing Company, Inc.
387 Park Avenue South, New York, N.Y. 10016
© 1994 by Wolf Moondance
Additional illustrations © 1994 by Jim Sharpe
Distributed in Canada by Sterling Publishing
% Canadian Manda Group, P.O. Box 920, Station U
Toronto, Ontario, Canada M8Z 5P9
Distributed in Great Britain and Europe by Cassell PLC
Villiers House, 41/47 Strand, London WC2N 5JE, England
Distributed in Australia by Capricorn Link (Australia) Pty Ltd.
P.O. Box 6651, Baulkham Hills, Business Centre, NSW 2153, Australia
Manufactured in the United States of America
Printed and bound in Hong Kong
All rights reserved

Sterling ISBN 0-8069-0364-3

Acknowledgments

There are many people who played a key role in my ability to see beyond and remember the vision of Rainbow Medicine. My heart-filled thanks go to these people: to my grandfather for his steadfast abandonment of my mother; to the faith healer for his empty promises; to the junk dealer who stole my marbles; to the elementary school teacher who refused to answer my questions; to my father for his unrelenting intensity; to my high school English teacher for her narrow-minded arrogance; to the stewards of war who murdered my friends and my president; and most of all to those people in the churches whose fear of life makes them unwilling to know Jesus the two-legged.

And my deepest thanks also go to the following people, who have made my earth walk richer and enabled me to tell the tale of the Wolf: to my mom and other moms, Crazy Helen, Alice, Mom Bilbe, and Lenie; to my guardian angels Dock Williams, Anita and Hawk; to my yellow eyes Sharon White Arrow, Susan Singing Earth Bear, Katherine and Wade, to my sister Betty Susan Conwell, and to Joanne Granny Jo; to Grandmother Big Nancy for her humor; to Lael and Sheila Anne for seeing my vision; to those who taught the growth; to my half side; to those who carry the colors and walk the Rainbow Path; to my ancestors and elders, Grandfather, Grandmother, Great Spirit.

Aho.

Purpose

Rainbow Medicine is a vision given to me by Great Spirit. It is a truth that I live, teachings that I have learned to understand, a way to build a road of existence. It is a path that ties into many other connections called the Rainbow. As I write *Rainbow Medicine*, twenty years of my life have gone into its preparation. I have had many students, and much time has been spent in prayer and hard work to see this vision come to a reality.

I was born and raised in Oklahoma and am of English, Osage and Cherokee descent. I am very proud to be an American and to walk as a Hollow Bone. To have the ability to be a visionary and a teacher of sacred truth, this is what I have gained from Rainbow Medicine. When I look at the life of Native Americanism through my mother's walk on the earth, I see sadness. I see a life that was deprived of its natural way, connecting her with shamanism; she was denied this and raised as a Catholic.

The cycle of shamanism is passed on through the blood. It is a gift to the children of those who walk before them. When I was a little Hollow Bone, I was walking with the gift of shamanism, but my family was deprived of the Native ways, as many were. The missionary teachings we were given instead had nothing to do with true Christianity—nothing to do with Christ. They seemed instead to deprive us of our teachings in the ways of being able to achieve our vision and to know our direction and path. When an individual's belief of shamanism is altered and a foreign religion is placed in the heart, one's communication with Great Spirit and nature is altered; it causes a dilemma leading to alcoholism and abuse. Each of us that walks our Earth walk has a certain amount of abuse that we deal with every day. Through my years of living a mixed life of two worlds, both white and native, I have seen many types—and experienced many types—of abuse.

My life is dedicated to Rainbow Medicine, a vision brought to me when I was five, which I share with you now. I hope that what I write is good for all people. It is necessary to know your way home. It is necessary to find your path and make your life as comfortable as you can.

In shamanism there is a great deal of individualism. It is built on individual spirituality. We as people are taught to herd and become like cattle, to follow and do as we're told. The path of walking alone as an individual is a very scary thing. We are taught to hold on, to be greedy and jealous. This is a path of destruction, one that does not allow us to have our wholeness but allows the coyote to steal and trick our feelings.

In Rainbow Medicine I tell a powerful story—a tale of the Wolf, a way that I walk with pride—from my father's people, the Wolf Clan. It is a way that I live every day through the eyes of a wolf that walks as a human. The Wolf is the keeper of the path, the way home. In the old ways, one leaves through the South, follows the Milky Way and finds the way to Spirit World. I feel that this speaks of walking through the emotions.

The story I am about to tell you is real. It weaves in and out of shamanic journeying, which takes us into an altered state of consciousness, a place of reality that I have experienced and where I know my way. I live my life the medicine way every day, according to what I hear from Great Spirit. And those who choose to walk with me hear my words. Sometimes they are very sharp, for my teeth are long and they bite hard. And sometimes they are soft and gentle, as my tongue caresses the hair of each of you.

The ways of the medicine path are hard. They bring you to your own truth. Set in the ways of the light, you may often have to turn your back to the dark. This can become very painful, for it closes doors. But as a door closes, you step into a new realm. If you keep your eyes in front of you, you will see the new realm, one of adventure within.

The purpose of Rainbow Medicine is to allow us to have an individual healing. Grandfather has given us a challenge to live each day a good way. It is my intention that *Rainbow Medicine* tie together the experiences of the spirit world and the real world, and show the way home.

Aho.

· 1 ·
The Path

Before me I see the path. It's a familiar path, with familiar smells, cool and inviting. I feel my feet walking on the path. It's a pleasure to touch the dirt. I hear the winged ones sing their evening song. The rock people greet me as I step on them and I listen to each of their lessons.

The round rocks bring me the knowledge of smoothness—the ability to roll with things. I hear their words—clearer and clearer: "When life is rough, we roll gently, tumbling to and fro on the terrain. Once we were the sharp ones. Once we had points and edges. But as the terrain became our way, we became smooth. Now we simply roll along, bumping and spinning and turning and bouncing.

"It's easy," the smooth ones say. "The way of the smooth rocks is easy. Take these lessons with you and when you see us, always remember that it's easy."

I hold one of them in my hand. It is orange. I feel the orange color—the earth in my hand—the many, many years of rolling across the terrain. I keep that in mind, that smooth, round, orange rock. I continue to walk as the rock people speak. I see a rock that is square and flat.

"With me, you could build a house. I'm a foundation—a rock that holds things solid and can be stood upon. In the earth walk, when you build a foundation, it must be solid. It speaks of intentions. We the flat rocks are those you build upon. We are your intentions. We hold the planning within us."

"This is quite an unusual place, rock. Where am I?"

"Oh, you're on the path and we are the greeters. We are the teachers, the ones who tell you the history. We're the ancient recorded knowledge of stories vast. Vast stories. Many of us lie ahead of you in your earth walk."

On my left I hear giggling, twinkling sounds of laughter. I look and there are rows of crystal within the granite rock.

"We are the crystal people and we are known as the laughing ones. We speak happiness to your journey. We magnify the strength of the granite. Strength is held together with laughter and joy. It isn't a solemn thing to be strong. It's a joyous combination of laughter, lightheartedness and the intention that the square ones speak of."

I step upon a sharp rock, one that twists my ankle.

"Ohhh, you have met the lesson. The rock of paying attention, the sharp one, the one with the edge."

Now the pain in my ankle is stronger than the lesson. I begin to cry.

"Crying will do you no good," says the Sharp One. "Crying is just the release of feeling sorry. It's just sadness for the self. Look at me in a different way and look at the pain with a different face. What you're doing, you've been taught. You were thinking of intention, going along in a smooth way, listening to the joy of the sparkling ones. Then you stepped on me and you're sad. It is not sadness that you need. It is alertness. Where was your mind, Little One? Where was your mind?"

"I was paying attention to the lessons," I say, "and admiring their beauty. It's fascinating, this path—full of mystery."

"Oh, you're right about that," says the Sharp One. "And that's what I'm here for. The sharp rocks will remind you that the unknown is all around you. You step in levels. Go inside the path on the first level and it goes deeper. Each lesson after that goes deeper within until finally you come to the core. And even there, the lessons spiral deeper. So this place that you're going, you're there now.

"To understand spiritual intention and insight is the knowledge of the rock people. Within each of us is the story of yesterday. Here, in the spirit world, you find the answers and achieve spiritual insight."

"Answers! What answers? Do you have the answers to everything?" I ask.

"Will I know everything, like how butterflies are made and why kittens play? Do you have the answers to all those things?"

"We all have the answers to those things. They lie recorded within our lives, for we are the fragments and pieces of those things." I hear this answer from a very odd rock that is in front of me. It is smooth, thick and round. A ray of light comes from it. I get closer.

"Wow! You have a hole all the way through you."

"Yes. I do," the rock replies. "I am One Who Knows. The hole is a place that takes you within my knowledge and through which you can see. Take me back into the world, on your earth walk. When you're lost and lonely and can't see your way, hold me up, look through the hole and pay very close attention. You'll become aware of everything around you and you'll understand where you are."

"I'm going to look through you right now," I reply, "because this is a really different kind of place. I've never seen such beauty. I've never been on a path where rocks could talk. I'm just a little person. It's hard for me to remember all this."

"Oh, there's no such thing as a 'little person' here. Little is the size. Little is a place where you are in comparison. Here, within these lessons, is grand wisdom. You have the space to learn all there is, because each moment of existence is a part of us. Each tree person, each human, each four-legged, each winged one—all are a part of the earth mother and the vastness of our knowledge. We go from coast to coast and around the world in our assignments on the earth walk. While you're on this place known as Earth, you have us to teach you lessons. I am one who knows. When you look for a rock with a hole in it, you are looking for balance—for the ability to focus—for seeing into the spirit world and drawing knowledge from it."

Another rock is shaped like a pyramid. It has a point at the top. It is shiny and smooth. As I come closer I notice swirling colors and patterns. It is soft yellow and white, with lines as if painted by a brush.

"I'm interesting, aren't I? I'm an agate—a pyramid agate. I'm one who has knowledge. My name is Point. Sometimes they speak of me as the Pointed One.

"I sit on the square. My sides are of equal value and they come to a point. Every lesson, every teaching, has four corners and four sides. It gets to the top, then it's at point—the front line.

"Get to the point. That will take the fear away! There will be times in your life, always, when you're scared. It's a normal, two-legged thing to be. Fear is a way of knowing. It's a necessary emotion that tells you to back up and take a look. It tells you when to jump and when to stand still. Listen to your fear, and then get to the point of it. When you're there—right there at the top where my head is—you're in a place of power. You're in control.

"These are my teachings. When you *listen* to your fear you can understand the *lesson* your fear speaks to. Then you gain power, and this takes the fear away."

Whew! My head is spinning. Listening to Point is a hard thing to do. It is hard to understand what takes fear away.

Walking further, I see purple rocks and blue ones. I see green ones. Oh, the green ones are beautiful—a rich, dark, deep green.

"We are Emeralds," they say. We speak of knowledge that you will remember always. You have the ability to grow, to see beauty. This is our message. Explore. Look at life as an adventure."

The emeralds remind me of a town, a whole city, the way they are shaped. "Come in," they say, and I feel myself go in. I become a part of their city, and I am surrounded by rich, deep green.

The energy of the green is movement—change—and it spirals around me. I feel a relaxation come over me. Worry and tension leave my body. I am changing. Fears are releasing. Acceptance is at hand. Tremendous transformation is taking place. I am no longer the same.

I Hear the Rapid Beat of the Drum Calling Me Back.

These words you have read are real. They are true within my understanding of existence as a two-legged and as a spirit. They were given to me in the vision of Rainbow Medicine.

Let me describe the word *medicine* to you. First, of course, there are the ordinary definitions: medicine is something you get in a jar that cures you, some little pill that makes you better, an ointment that changes things, surgery that alters and rearranges.

Medicine is also discipline. It is an application of faith with the truth of what is so for you (for example, how your individual chemistry lines up with the chemistry of the product you place in your body). Medicine is finding vibrational frequencies and reading them. Medicine is understanding why we do what we do and using this knowledge on our path so that we may achieve companionship, relationship and responsibility.

Rainbow Medicine

Sacred Tools

Sacred tools for ceremonial use are items that help you to connect, to focus and to interpret your feelings. They can be anything with special meaning to you. In the medicine walk, sacred tools are often drums, rattles, feathers, beads, stones and herbs. Objects such as prayer beads, crosses, candles, candelabras and incense are also considered sacred tools.

Sacred tools are also known as "transitional tools," because they assist in the transition through. You may choose to use certain tools for all of your life. A specific tool may be important to you for a while and then, when you know that you are finished with it, you are free to move on to another tool. Sacred tools must be treated with respect: keep them in a safe place and clean them before use (and sometimes after) by smudging or immersing in sea saltwater.

Anything that you connect with, learn from, and that speaks to your heart can be a sacred tool. Marriage, graduations, births and funerals may even be considered sacred tools. If you look at all events as sacred or transitional tools, you can move clearly and cleanly from one to another, learning lessons and sitting in the sacredness of each.

To sum it up, sacred tools assist you in setting yourself to make prayer in a good way. They help you understand that a vision is the purest contact with Great Spirit that a human being can have, and in that vision is the Great Mystery always.

Smudging

A powerful tool that is used in contemporary shamanism is the ceremony of smudging, which clears the etheric realm. This is the energy field surrounding your body that is known as "your space." Your feelings extend up to 100 feet beyond your "physical body," and make up part of the etheric realm. This field collects energies that enable you to make decisions. In this space you feel such sensations as the wind blowing, temperature, harsh or soft words, the feelings and intentions of others. When someone steps into this space, they are stepping into your etheric realm. It is necessary to balance your etheric field with a cleansing from time to time, especially before you begin any ceremonial, visioning or journey work.

To smudge, place pieces of sage or cedar or both in a shell (abalone is most often used) or a fireproof clay bowl. Light the herbs, blow out any flame, and allow the smoke to rise. Move the smoke in a clockwise and upward motion, using either your hand or a feather. In this way you may smudge yourself, another person, a sacred tool or any space.

The sacred smoke of cedar and sage provide centering, balancing, soothing and cleansing positive ions that bond with the negative ions that have collected in etheric fields. What is felt as "negative energy" is thus neutralized. This causes a cleansing within the etheric realm that penetrates to the physical level. As you breathe in the fragrance, you feel healing positive ions cleansing any toxins that might be present in your physical form.

Smudging brings you to your center, enabling you to perform other ceremonies in "a good way." "A good way" is anything that creates positive ions, positive energy, and a balancing force that enables you to walk your path healthy and whole.

The Need for Journalling

A journal is a tool that you use to keep your balance, to look at where you are, where you've been, and where you're going. Your journal is essential for keeping the pieces of sacred intervention that you are given. By recording them in a journal, you will be able to recall what the mind thinks and then seems to let go of—lets slip away.

Journalling meets the need to have a safe space to share your feelings, organize your data and study the things that you bring back from your visioning and sacred experiences.

A journal can be as simple as a three-ring binder or a plain tablet, or it can be as elaborately decorated as you like. It is something that is private and should be kept private. Be aware that anyone else, looking at it, can create barriers and boundaries, intruding upon the safety of your inner self. Therefore, to be in balance, you must trust that the people in your presence will respect your journalling.

The Process of Finding Your Path

These ceremonies may be done at any time of the day. Find a quiet space where you won't be disturbed, where there is no electricity, no noise, no interruptions, no four-legged to run through your sight.

Acknowledging Your "Life Path"

Tools: *Cornmeal; journal and pen; sacred tools of your choice*

Build a cornmeal circle.

Begin by honoring the sun—starting in the east of your circle, where the sun rises. Standing in the east, raise a pinch of cornmeal above you, giving thanks to the spirits of the east, and to Great Spirit for all that comes from the east.

Make a circle seven feet (2.1m) in diameter by sprinkling the cornmeal clockwise towards the south. (If you have chosen an inside spot, you may wish to spread a large blanket on which to build your circle.) Once you come to the south, pause and honor the south in the same way.

Continue forming the cornmeal circle, stopping to honor the west and the north.

As you come back to the East Gate, step inside the circle, taking with you your journal and a pen. Once you step inside, do not leave the circle until you have found your path, as described here.

1. **Centering.** Take a deep breath in through your nose and out through your mouth. Center yourself by sitting in any position that you have learned, using any breathing method that you have learned. I recommend extending your arms to the heavens and honoring the Creator—Grandmother/Grandfather Spirit—and any personal deities and spirits that teach you of a spirit way. Breathe in and out four times, relax and clear your mind. Become focused on the process of finding your path.

2. **Sorting out your path.** Open your journal and put down the heading, "Paths that I have journeyed and the Path that I am on." List the

experiences that have led to the path you are on, including such aspects as schooling, career, marriage, alcoholism, drug abuse, anger, love, searching, seeking. Try to identify where you are on the path. There are many avenues to your path; list each one, and go deeply into how you feel you are doing.

> *Example:* I am walking the path of being a Grand Teacher. I have dedicated my life to teaching spirituality and shamanism. I am walking the path of acceptance and commitment to Christ. I walk the path of responsibility for the four-legged that I come upon and the winged ones that might need my assistance. I am on the path of Rainbow Medicine. I honor the teachings of the Seven Sacred Stars and the color that holds the words of each.

List the avenues to your path and get them clear in your mind.

3. **Honoring your ceremonies of intention.** Take a moment to determine where you set your intentions to begin these avenues. What were the ceremonies? Were they graduation ceremonies, or ceremonies of rites of passage? What things have you done that enable you to stand in a good way and know that you are what you say?

> *Examples:* A wedding, a formal commitment to the ministry, a commitment to the teaching field, a commitment to be a healer.

Look at these different achievements and appreciate them by taking a deep breath and thinking how they will be for you. Know that you are the person in charge of your life and that these ceremonies set avenues in motion for you to follow as life paths.

Check to see that you have listed all the goals of your vision that you wish to live.

At the moment when you have listed each avenue that you are walking, give back to the earth what it has given to you. Take a deep breath and scatter cornmeal on the ground in the circle around you, in honor of those things.

4. **Choosing your life path.** What is the path that you wish to follow for your entire earth walk? Start a new heading, "My Life Path," and list the avenues that you choose to be on.

It is most important that the things you do be personal to yourself. Think them out, organize them and understand them in a good way. For whether they are traditional or contemporary, it is your choice.

If you have the honor, the ability and the chance to follow the ways of your grandparents on your earth walk and to listen to traditions, think about those now. Sit in your sacred site and think about your grandparents, your aunts and uncles, your traditions; the Sunday gatherings, the daily and weekly teachings; the things that go on within a home that make it a home. Draw from those strengths and think about your memories—even arguments and quarrels and "bad" things, as you see them. When you let go of your anger, they too will become your traditions. For they are avenues that are constantly with you, teaching you the ways, the traditions, of your family.

If yours is a contemporary path, you will be on your own to listen to Great Spirit and come to fullness with your own path, which is new and opens the door to new and different experiences. No one before you has followed your path. You will set a new way of action in motion.

Now, as you ceremonially choose your spiritual path, keep in mind always that the rainbow is beneath your feet—that you cross the earth walk with many different nations, with many different colors, many bloods, broken beliefs and solid ones, fractions of knowledge and wholeness of knowledge.

> *Example:* I am on the Rainbow Path. There are many avenues: I walk with the knowledge of the sun, the seven stars and the moon, which is my vision. I accept the path that I walk as a teacher of spirituality and a Grand Teacher of contemporary shamanism. The path before me I accept as a mystery, one that is always in the hands of Great Spirit. I accept the path of the teachings of Jesus Christ—brought to us by the missionary teachings that opened my eyes to the vision quest that Jesus lived. I honor all of these things as my path.

5. **Accepting your chosen path.** When you have finished organizing your path list, take a deep breath in through your nose and hold it. Let the thoughts inside your mind settle. Breathe out through your mouth. Continue breathing in and out like that and feel good. Enjoy a warm feeling of the sun shining on you. Experience a deep feeling of understanding the path that lies ahead of you. Finish your journal work by closing with your statements and feelings about your decisions and intentions to follow your personal spiritual path. Speak them aloud, with strength and assurance.

> *Example:* I, Wolf, look forward to the path that I have chosen and been given through the vision of the sun and the stars and the moon. I recognize that I am accountable and responsible for

each step of my earth walk, understanding that I and I alone make my decisions. I choose the light in my life. I choose to hear the voice of Great Spirit and all that have gone before me. I will walk towards the great white light, to sit in the presence of All That Is, Creator, Grandfather/Grandmother, the Great What Is, the Great Mystery, God our Father. Aho.

6. **The power of closing.** When you end your writing, set in motion your determination by using the power of ending. Make a closing statement such as "Aho," or "So be it," or "Amen." Make a strong closing with a clean, solid word.

7. **Giving thanks.** While standing in your circle, take a deep breath in through your nose, hold it and *know* that you have a life path. Let the breath go. Continue to breathe in and out, knowing that your breath will stabilize you as you walk on your path. As you prepare to leave your circle through the east gate, give thanks to Creator for what you have received.

Journal about your path—your actions and your feelings—every day. With every journal entry allow yourself to become intrigued, enriched, enlightened and illuminated by the beauty that is you on your path.

The "Journey Path"

Journeying is a unique shamanic means of travel. It takes you inside your mind—past imagination, past fantasy and into the realm of journey—into the spirit realm. To access these worlds, it is helpful to visualize a path. This journey path will become very familiar to you, very comfortable, and whenever you do your journey work, you will seek it out. It may always stay the same, or it may change in shape, size, color, lighting or surroundings. No matter how it changes, you will always recognize it as your personal journey path that takes you into the shamanic realm of spirit where there are lessons and teachings, comfort and guides.

When you feel yourself rising, you are travelling to the upper world. There you will meet with teachers and receive your lessons. Spirit guides will come to you here, offering you their comfort and assistance. These energies are very real, always to be respected and honored.

When you are centered, stay in the middle realm, standing outside of yourself. Here, you are able simply to look inside yourself, recognizing your wants and your needs.

When you feel yourself descending, you are travelling to the lower world. You are going back into the realm of fantasy and imagination, where things may be animated, cartoon-like, detached, and possibly even frightening.

Discovering Your Journey Path

Needed: *Journal and pen; sacred tools of your choice*

1. **Seeing the path.** Sit or lie in a comfortable position. Take four breaths in through the nose and out through the mouth. Close your eyes. Before you, you'll see a path. This is your "Journey Path." Describe it in your journal. Feel your feet upon its surface, bend down and touch it. Describe its color and substance, how narrow or wide, the character of the lighting. Describe the surroundings. Note any sounds, sights and smells that are associated with this path. For example, the sound of tinkling bells, the glint of crystals, the scent of roses, jasmine, or sage.

2. **Following the path.** Now follow your path and begin to see it as you know it in your life. Feel the depth of each avenue. See your commitments and your responsibilities. See your accountability. Understand that you have set your intentions on these different avenues.

   While you're on this path, you'll be aware of many energies around you. They are guides, lessons and teachers that you need. See them clearly, feel them strongly and hold them in your mind. Bring all of this knowledge back in whole formulated sentences that are clean and clear to you. Record them in your journal.

3. **Fork in the path.** Be still for a moment. Before you there is a fork in the path. You have a choice. Look at it. Turn and look behind you and see the path you have taken up to here. Stand still and look beneath your feet. You have the choice of going back into what you know is comfortable (maybe not best, but comfortable). You can choose to stay where you're standing. You can take the straight path ahead of you into more of what is. Or you can take the fork and go a different way. You choose. And you experience the choice.

4. **Returning from the journey.** Hear the rapid sound of a drum, beating fast and intense, calling you back to your reality. Come back from your journey. Come back to your middle world, to the place where you are in your two-legged walk. Know that your personal

journey path always leads you back to the realm of the physical, back to your earth walk. Feel your spirit settling in your body. Open your eyes.

5. **Journal your experience.** Describe how it feels to look backwards, to stand still, to follow the straight path or to choose another branch. You now have the tools and the opportunity to take a ceremonial walk on your journey path at any time, to follow the road of the spiritual life that lies within your spirit, to access experiences that shape your life in the physical realm, to listen and learn from Great Spirit. Using these teachings, you may alter your earth walk daily and shape your "life path."

Spiritual journey work should not be done under the influence of alcohol or drugs of any kind. Your diet should be sound and your sugars in balance. Good physical health and sobriety are essential to attain spiritual heights. A commitment to physical well-being is necessary in order to undertake spiritual growth. The adventure of a shamanic journey is a high in itself and need not be tampered with or adjusted by artificial stimulants.

Aho.

· 2 ·
The Vision

A garden is where I stand. There are carrots and corn, lettuce and beets. The squash grows; so do the pumpkins and watermelons. I turn to the fruit, to the strawberries and blackberries—to the fruit trees standing with the pear people, the peach people and the apples. I breathe in their aromas and hold them as a child. The grapes—I eat them. I feel their strength. And then I hear their words.

"You have come here to live with us for a reason. We, the grape people, the purple ones, hold the keys to ancient wisdoms. We have many purposes in our earth walk. We become the sweet treat you have in the morning, that you throw down your throat on a piece of bread as you hurry out the door. But we're more than that. We're round. We have no beginning and no end, as your day will have. Because it is morning and you have awoken, it seems the beginning, but the morning is simply a part of the cycle. And we represent that. We're round, with a story to tell.

"Stop in the morning and listen to what we have said—grasp the feeling of our wisdom. Take time to understand that the balance of the morning meal sets the pace for the rest of the day."

I sense fullness from my visit with the grape people. I turn and walk toward the flowers. There are rows upon rows of them. Freshness, beauty, color, intensity are their ways. Butterflies dance and songs are sung. I listen to the tunes of the little winged ones, the dragonflies, the butterflies, the bee people. It is a marvelous world I have entered.

I hear a very small voice coming from a gathering of petal people. A strong red rose is speaking of its origin, teaching the truth of its ways.

"Now, you know that confidence isn't a thing that you just go and get someplace. You have to believe. You can't grow without confidence. You must believe in the sun, that warm rays will come and that you will grow."

It seems as if the flowers are in school, all taking in the words of the confident rose.

"We, the roses, have always been strong ones. We have thorns; we have the ability to keep the two-legged in line if they carelessly pick our blossoms. We're not just ornaments—we are food supply. We're the spirit of giving, but we're also the ones that teach the lessons of paying attention.

"Thistles teach lessons when the two-legged strike out and call some of us weeds. You'll have to forgive these two-legged. They love to see and smell some of us, especially when the spring comes. They like our lavender brothers and the strong scents of the carnation and honeysuckle that linger in the air. They want certain ones of us around. Those of us that don't fit, they call weeds. Weeds are just misplaced flowers. Thistles, dandelions and nettles—so often referred to as weeds by the two-legged—are much more than that. The two-legged struggle and fight and make fools of themselves trying to get rid of us. They yank us out of the ground and throw us in a pile. They bare the ground to nothingness, then they put us in rows and plant us like they want us. They organize life so that they have control. And they do the same thing to themselves. They argue and fight and yank each other from the ground.

"Now I, the red rose, speak to you this morning in the sun, so listen and pay careful attention to Grandfather's wishes. We speak of balance, of creativity. We provide knowledge, and the lessons of growth. We have the wisdom to understand that the creepy crawlies and the small winged ones— the ants, bees, butterflies and hummingbirds—help make our next generation.

"So, you petalled ones, this small two-legged has listened to school today and has heard lessons of mystery. Perhaps respect is at hand."

I walk on and come upon a pond, small and quiet. A lily pad floats on the surface. The sun shimmers on the water and catches my eye. There dances a sparkling spirit—a tiny, vibrant, glistening being.

"You come here to the garden to listen to the ways. Know that the stories the petal people tell happen here every day. Know also that they are your medicine. Time is a reality on your earth walk, so when you go back, remember the words of confidence. Take the lessons of each petal that falls. And remember that we are all part of the cycle."

I walk on to a place of soft green grass. Barefoot, I feel this grass and it speaks to me.

"Sit with us. Lie with us. Take a nap on us. It's time to rest here on us— we're thick, like a carpet or bed. We're the grass people, that nurture and feed the four-legged. We're the ones that provide rest and comfort from the cold of the night. Come lie down and take a nap. Be with us."

The grass is cool beneath my feet. I lie down and feel the sun shining on me. "What a wonderful place," I think, "where flowers teach and grass talks."

I go deeper into the space of the grass and my little body relaxes. I am no longer one who skins knees and chases kittens and doesn't like to take vitamins. I am no longer a two-legged who needs to do chores. I am feeling safe with the grass people, who speak lessons.

"When you walk in your world, you must walk with your vision. You must know where you go. You may always come back to us and lie down and draw strength from the soil and the soft ones that comfort you. But on this earth walk, little one, remember your purpose.

"It is with intention that life begins beyond this earth in the land of Grandmother/Grandfather, Great Spirit, Great Mystery. Now, as you rest, we give to you your vision."

Lying in the green grass, on my back, I focus on the sky. There I see the sun—with four lines on each side—top and bottom, left and right. It is bright yellow, intensely yellow. Below it, I see a blue crescent moon. Between this setting moon, starting at the top and spiralling down, I see a red star, an orange star, a yellow star, a green star, a blue star, a purple star, and a burgundy star. I see the sun and the moon and the stars.

It is grand, because behind each of these stars it seems as if there are millions more—billions and trillions of twinkling points of color.

"Grass people, what have I seen?" I ask. "What are this sun and moon and these stars about?"

The grass people laugh, and they say, "Well, it's the sun and the moon and everything in between. It's your path. It's your vision. Grasp it and hold it dear. Hang on to it. It's come to heal the fear. Remember it and always keep it near."

I walk further down the path. Smells of smoke. A teepee, with door open. I stand looking. What is this world—these houses I see, with poles and things blowing in the breeze—bells, feathers and beads. So much color. The bright sun. I begin to dance. Then I see clouds in the sky, white ones on one side and black ones on the other. The clouds grow thicker until I see their faces and they begin to speak.

"There is great medicine, much to learn. Yes, that's right. My name is White Cloud. I am the teacher of sacredness, the teacher of respect. The one who brings you understanding of the light."

There is nothing across from me. Then I see that what looked like nothing is a big, black, dark cloud looking at me with angry green eyes.

"Yes," it says. "I'm nothing. With shades of pain to endure. Understand that pain will be the process you remember. I'll bring you confusion and temptation. My lining is made of lies and the need to manipulate. I bring the times when the truth will be too hard. Breathe my air. Pull it deep inside of your life."

And laughter, like thunder, echoes in my mind.

"No. No. Don't listen," says White Cloud. "Pull away. Come and be with us, the white ones, the light. Let me show you what's inside of us."

I choose to become one with the white clouds. I float and spiral. A soft mist is all around me. Vary pale pink, pale orange, pale yellow, pale green and pale blue. There is pale purple and pale burgundy—all the colors so soft. They swirl around me, spinning, spiralling. I float in the soft rays of a great white light. Within the light I see a grandfather, a gentle man motioning to me. He extends his hand and in it is a piece of red clay. He extends his other hand, and in it is a piece of wood.

"This is male and female, this wood and clay. The beginning and the end."

He puts the two together and forms a circle from the wood and the clay. From that circle comes smoke.

"Some people call the smoke legends," he says. "Some call it stories, others call it prayers. You have seen this circle of smoke."

I watch the smoke rise.

"On the earth walk, the male and the female are everything. From the mother and father comes the child. This gives existence in an earth way. Here, within the land of spirit, they are a symbol to connect you and prepare you for your earth walk. Always honor and respect your vision as you walk. Always listen to your vision—and watch."

I look into the pale smoke and I see the sun with the four sets of four lines. I see the seven stars and the moon. I hear the old man say, "This is your prayer. Pray it as you believe it. Believe it as you pray it."

"I don't know how to do that," I reply.

"You don't know how to pray? Prayer is the connecting point between spirit and the physical. When you don't pray, you have no communication. Prayer is the place where you stand in total openness—where you speak of your earthly needs and fears. Where you receive your spiritual fortitude. You must stand in that place now and pray."

I watch the smoke rise as it spins around and around. "It's simple," he says. "Ask that your prayer draw out your fears and then cast them into the smoke, where they disappear. Simply say, 'This is my prayer.'"

I Hear the Rapid Beat of the Drum Calling Me Back.

Vision Feather

Needed: *Feather of any type; 100% cotton red cloth; a white bead; string; tobacco*

The cloth is used as a wrapping on the bottom of the feather to honor and represent the good Red Road. The white bead represents Great Spirit.

Wrap a ¼-inch (6mm) strip of the red cloth around the bottom stem of the feather. Tie it on with the string and hang the white bead on one of the ties.

Focus your attention on the feather while getting balanced. As you look directly at the feather, your mind will begin to see images and hear sounds that are the vision. Listen and watch carefully as you use the feather. Record in your journal all you see and hear while working with the vision feather.

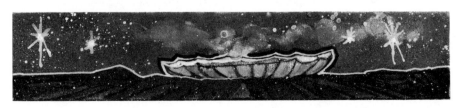

The Process of Achieving Your Vision

Receiving a vision is empowering—take it seriously. When Great Spirit blesses you and gives you a glimpse of your life, carry it with sacredness and remember it every day. Analyze it and it will open doors for you.

A vision is the calling of Great Spirit. Many have said that the vision you are given becomes your way of life. It puts the pieces together and allows you to know what is so for you.

A vision is not just sight, nor thoughts alone, nor spirit only. When a vision comes to you it is like a butterfly floating in the sky. It is the miracle of transformation.

My vision was clear to me when I was five years old. Childhood is that way. Now, my vision is an image of my path. It is my story—the sun and the moon and everything in between.

Your vision may be something as simple as a tree with two birds. It happens when you reach into the spirit world—Great Spirit touches you, and you have faith. However simple your vision may be, remember that your power comes by living it.

Following your vision is a choice that allows you to know yourself in a rich and full way. As you unlock the doors of your vision, a self-dedication grows. Walk your vision. Know the truth and take the chance. Reach for the moon, sing the song—and the joy within your vision.

The Relationship of "Path" and "Vision"

Your "path" is the link between you and Great Spirit. It is necessary to have a path in order for Great Spirit to gift you with a "vision." When a true link is in place, Creator speaks to you in many ways. By remaining dedicated to the disciplines and commitments of your path, you continually strengthen this link and your vision becomes stronger.

How to Recognize a Vision

A vision is communication from Great Spirit. Your mind is the receiving device.

When you have a vision, it will come to you as a symbol, an animated picture, a poem, a song. It will haunt your mind. This is the way you know that you have had a vision. The "haunting" feeling becomes a calling, opening the door for great adventure.

Visioning is never connected with physical actions such as sexual intercourse, eating, exercising, or cleaning the body. The process of visioning is an adventure of its own, a quest that needs to be structured and organized. It is important to ceremonially set yourself apart in a very quiet, restful, peaceful way—to nurture yourself with as much beauty as the earth mother has to offer.

Your Personal Vision

Early on you may receive one definite over-arching vision, which you will recognize as your personal vision. Or, you may receive bits and pieces over time. Either way, every bit that you receive adds to the vision. In this way your vision remains fluid and it grows as you grow.

Preparing to Receive Visions

Laying the groundwork for visioning is vitally important. See your vision as a seed and yourself as a garden. Know that a garden needs to be tilled—the earth must be made ready for planting. If you have prepared the soil of yourself, your vision seeds will flourish and you will reap the bounty.

This section does not take you through a specific ceremony. Instead it prepares you, leaving you ready to receive your visions when and where they come to you.

Becoming ready and whole

1. **Spiritual understanding.** To achieve spiritual understanding, it is necessary to organize your spiritual beliefs, to understand that you have the ability to set out a spiritual map that will allow you to achieve your vision. To do this, you need to understand your family beliefs and the traditional beliefs of your family bloodline, as well as the connections with those who have raised you. You need to understand these values in order to set your path in motion.

   I believe that all paths are of the same walk, serving the light or the absence of it. Will your vision be Christian in nature? Will it be Roman Catholic, Jewish, or Native American or any other religion or philosophy? Will it be of a far-off country? It is very important that you understand the path of your heritage that has brought you to your vision. The understanding of your spiritual background and the symbols within it enable you to read your vision and expand your knowledge of it.

2. **Emotional understanding.** There are six basic emotions, combinations of which produce what we know as feelings. The six emotions are: fear, anger, disgust, sadness, acceptance and joy.

Understand that your emotions speak to you for a valid reason. Knowing what is at the root of your feelings and accepting how you feel is essential. Anger, for example, can throw you totally off your path of light. Or you can draw motivation from your anger and recognize that your emotions have brought you to this place to learn lessons.

Journalling is a powerful tool. Write down the things that you're afraid of; the things that make you angry; the things that disgust you; the things that make you sad; the things that you accept in life; and the things that bring you joy.

The process of putting your emotions in order will prepare you to receive your vision.

3. **Physical understanding.** It is very important that your physical body be in good shape so that you may obtain, interpret, maintain and live a vision. At first the vision is given to you by Great Spirit. As you interpret it, the vision may, for example, take you around the world to gather the knowledge that you need to fulfill it. Maintaining and living your vision may also require great amounts of energy.

It is important that you be as healthy as you can be, eating proper meals in correct amounts, and having your body in a good way so that you have energy reserves for the thinking necessary to achieve a vision. It is also necessary to have an active exercise program so that you are in shape and prepared for the intensity that is within your vision.

I suggest that you deal with any alcohol and drug addictions, for these alter the process of the true vision. Substance abuse of any kind takes a toll on the body, and prevents you from hearing what your mind is receiving and projecting.

4. **Mental understanding.** Your mind is a recording unit—able to structure, organize, process, analyze, project, develop and administer orders to the central nervous system. When you understand this, you will allow yourself to receive and interpret your visions.

The human brain is made up of chemicals and matter that allow the mind to hold the magical mystery of the Great What Is, and to obtain the levels of knowledge that are necessary to reach your bliss. The cravings that we have as human beings are affected by the brain's needs. Once an addition has stimulated the brain to crave the source of that addiction, the need for balance is at hand. A mind that functions in a good way must have a constant sugar balance to avoid artificial highs and lows.

The brain must have a consistent supply of energy if the mind is to have the confidence needed to maintain balance, to perform creatively and to administer growth. This brings about your solid truth and allows you to seek out your wisdom.

If these things are to happen in a good way, then you need to understand the mind in its fullness. Look at the mind as a four-step circle—understand that it is chemicals, it is matter, it is a container of spirit and it is spirit. The more you understand about human anatomy and functioning, the more powerfully you will walk.

Setting the purpose—or intention—that supports your vision

1. **Go to the core** of what your vision will mean in your life. Outline what your vision is for.

   Example: My vision will place before me a picture, a map, a way to integrate my thinking. It will provide structure for my human existence. It will allow me to achieve the totality of my path. If at any time I pull away from this, I will be off my path and not connected to my vision. At that point I will be simply existing and could be very lost.

   Journalling the purpose of your vision opens the doors of reality and sets you on the path of fulfillment.

2. **Understand Dream.** We human beings are continually dreaming, since we exist only through the thought of Great Spirit. Being that dream is human existence as I see it. Reaching the level of understanding your vision as a daydream, as an active dream, as a dream come true, as a nightmare—any of these choices—will open doors to the stability needed to achieve your vision.

3. **Setting goals.** An outline will allow you to achieve the fullness of your vision. Draw your goals from these suggestions:

   • What brings you joy—refer to the journal work you have done in section 2, "Emotional Understanding."

   Example: My vision will bring humor, grace, beauty and balance to my life, allowing me to experience joy—to walk in the beauty way. My vision will allow me to have in my life and experience to the fullest all of these things that bring me joy . . . (list them).

   • Your commitment and responsibilities—refer to the journal work you did in chapter 1, "Life Path" (see pages 15–18).

Example: By following my vision, I will gain the strength, balance, creativity, growth, truth and wisdom necessary to meet my commitments and responsibilities . . . (list them).

- Your personal truths—what is so for you.

  Example: Knowing your grandparents and seeing them reflected in your parents. Taking this as a personal heritage that forms your platform. *Goal:* My vision will help me walk with this heritage and pass it on, in a circle that never ends.

  Example: Reading and gathering data. *Goal:* By following my vision, I will continue to gather information, realizing that I am not alone—that my knowledge is part of a circle of wisdom.

- Your spiritual choices. Refer to the journal work you did in chapter 1 under your "Life Path" and list the choices that you choose to follow.

  Example: My vision will allow me to continue to follow these, my spiritual choices . . . (list them).

When you have set out these goals, know that:

- You have done what is necessary to motivate yourself to follow your vision and to create space for it.
- You will see your vision as a dream unfolding, which will be an absolute delight.
- You will follow these goals, not losing sight of them—knowing that your vision keeps you on your path.
- You will achieve the purpose of your vision and you will allow the heart core of your vision to open doors, setting up new dreams and goals past this point.

4. **Discipline needed to achieve your vision.** Know that when you have received a vision, commitment is at hand. Commitment requires discipline. This doesn't have to be a scary word. Simply look at it as tapping into your innate desire to survive.

   I recommend that you put daily effort into the following suggestions. This is your life—it is worth the effort.

- Keep your vision constantly in your mind. This helps you to achieve new levels of understanding and to pull together glimpses and pieces of knowledge from other sources. In this way you enrich your vision, allowing it to grow.
- Allow your vision to become an adventure. Within vision lies the

value of your life and you have the opportunity to lay that value in order—which is to make your own choice, to know that you are the one who knows what you want. If you can believe in your choice, your wants and needs will be all you dream and quest for. Delight in the feeling of structuring, organizing, administrating—living—your vision.

- Recognize and celebrate your uniqueness. Following your vision allows you to be an independent unit of wholeness and totality. It also shows you how to interact with the people in your life without being co-dependent.
- Walk the actual walk—"talk your talk." By following your vision—which comes from Great Spirit—you know what is so for you. You have a road map to live by. This is the discipline necessary to explore and develop your human existence, so that you may look back in your eldership and see the complete circle of seeking, finding, organizing and living your vision.

Getting Help with Your Vision

1. **Find a teacher**—someone who is following a personal vision in a way that can be taught. This person should understand that visions exist, and be able to help you begin the visioning process. Be sure, when seeking teachers, that they are teaching from an understanding of their vision.
2. **Connect with a shaman**—one who is wise and knows, one who lives, teaches and shows a personal vision through his or her individuality. When you meet a shaman, you will know it, because you will see the vision in the person's walk; you will hear the vision in the person's words. They will project it in their teachings, in their healings, in the way that they live.

   When you meet a student of this person, you will be able to see reflections of the shaman in the student's life. When students come to the shaman, they are often able to see their own vision through the discipline and the goals of the shaman. This motivates them to look within their own lives and to restructure their personal goals and values.
3. **Accept the ceremonies of your heritage**, ceremonies that are presented to you by a parent or other family member, that are passed on to you. You have been gifted with these sacred rites from your own family, and from them you learn the structure within which you seek out your personal vision.

4. **Study with a visionary,** one who has been walking a vision each moment, each hour, each day for at least 25 years. Visionaries walk their talk in a very powerful medicine way. In addition to their personal visions, they are able to reach into the prophet realm and vision for others. Some would call them seers, clairvoyants or psychics, but I believe that a visionary can be looked at as a true medicine person, one whose medicine is vision. You will know these people by the fact that they will be able to gift you with an outline of your vision, thus giving you the ability to identify your heart's dream, your spirit's needs, your soul's yearning.

Where to Go to Experience Your Vision

1. **The family home or environment,** if this is a safe space. If so, your family would celebrate with you and feel it a great honor for you to have your vision in a good way.

    The support of family members is what makes the word "family" meaningful. Here you can see a total circle, starting with one person's need. Those in the family recognize that need and do what they are able to do in a good way to meet it.

2. **A place chosen by the teacher.** You and your teacher team together and plan for a structured vision quest. Your teacher might suggest that you go to a specific sacred space or to a quiet spot within his or her own retreat. You sit in a space and follow guidelines that are agreed upon by the two of you in partnership.

3. **A place chosen by the group leader.** Go to a site chosen by the group leader with group participation. There, in a safe space where you are being watched over and protected in a good way, you have the quietness, structure and safety necessary to obtain your vision.

4. **A place chosen by your own spirit.** Decide where you wish to go, be it the mountains, the desert, the ocean or a sacred retreat space. Sit by yourself in a quiet way with your journal. Draw from the deepest part of your spirit, asking Great Spirit with sincerity, and you will be given the thought that is the beginning of your vision.

    Journal any thoughts, ideas, symbols, pictures, colors, smells, sounds, harmonies, stories, words, poems, shapes, and—most importantly—feelings. Give thanks for these pieces of illumination.

    Having the ability to reach within yourself is the first step of shamanism. It is the ability to go within and to understand.

Aho.

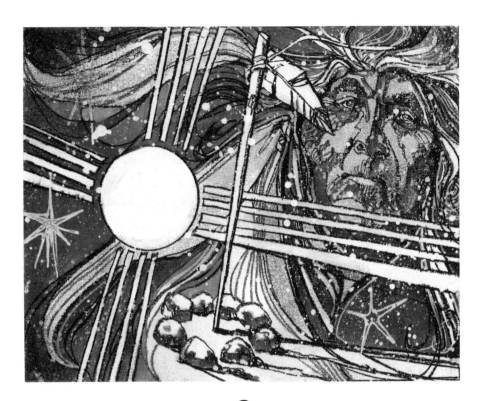

· 3 ·
The Sun

I begin to rise. I go higher and higher—up off the earth, out into the sky, where I feel myself flying, circling, diving. I can see all around me. Then I feel myself floating, as if I am in a parachute, but I'm not. Drifting through space, I realize that space IS—and that within space is color. I see it around me. I feel it as I float down. I realize that I am hanging on to a feather and that I have been floating with it through space. I land on the earth with the feather, and it connects itself to a pole. I stand looking at an enormous eagle feather.

"I am the feather of spirit," it says. "I represent Grandfather as you know him. I have come from the grandest and most majestic of all the great bald eagles. You are with me now and I am with you. Respect of my existence is what I ask. Do not let me fall to the ground. Do not let another harm me. Do not disrespect me. And never give me away without my story."

I stand in a space that is unfamiliar. "Where am I?" I ask the feather.

"You are in the center, at the point where the sun is direct. You are at the start. Around you is a story."

I look down and there I see a beautiful red rock, glistening and twinkling, shimmering. I look closely and see lines in this rock—a deeper rich red. Next to it is a rock that is orange. Next to it is a yellow one, followed by green, blue, purple and burgundy. The rocks form a circle; the red, the orange, the yellow, the green, the blue, the purple and the burgundy—a circle around the pole on which the feather hangs.

The purple rock speaks. "We are everything. You are standing in the center. In direct proportion. Everything that exists lies within the ancient wisdom here in this circle."

I begin to feel and to know. I sway with the breeze that blows the feather in a spiralling motion. I hear a soft flute, an inviting sound. I sit in the center, feeling the warm richness, the understanding of everything. This totalness is familiar.

The green rock speaks. "On your earth walk, as all two-legged do, you will experience pain. Center and become direct when that happens. Relate to this space where you are *now*. Understand. You're in the ebb and flow of growth when pain is at hand."

By now, I am tired. My head is spinning. I sense this spinning going from the ground to the top of my head and back and forth, up and down. I begin to relax.

"This is a good thing," the orange rock says. "You're beginning to understand balance. Here in the center there are no rules. Here, in the spirit world, there are no limits."

"Your personal wisdom is within this statement," says the purple rock. "You'll need this wisdom, as a two-legged, to understand the sun. To understand that there are many suns, to understand all of them. You must also come to understand pain. What caused it? Why did it happen? How did it happen? Where did it come from? You'll be seeking answers to all these things. You'll have to take every twist and turn of the river."

Laughter rings out of the rock so loudly it seems to echo off of a nearby canyon wall. Then a soft, swishing wind blows through my mind.

"Settle and focus. Right here, on the line," is the advice of the burgundy rock.

A still, deep quiet comes over me. I begin to relax and become one with this center, this spot of focus. Sitting in the circle, I look up at the feather that floats in the wind.

"You have brought me here for a reason, feather. I know that around me are lessons, and I listen."

I take a deep breath in and out. I relax and let go of my fear. I know that answers are here within me. The qualities of fire, earth, air, water, moon, sun, stars and mystery. The keys lie here within confidence and balance. I think of creativity and growth, truth, wisdom and impeccability.

"You see, if you just move over, just a little, everything is always different," says the yellow rock. "If you look at it from behind, it's different from the front. This is the mastery of creativity. The realization is that it is all just different perceptions and angles. This is yours to grasp within the center, within the sun."

"Am I on the sun?" I ask.

I look around. There is nothing but quietness. It seems as if I'm standing in space. Yet there is the circle of rocks, the pole, the feather and me. An absence of feeling closes in around me. I stay in the center, wondering where I am and what I am doing.

"Answers, I'm seeking, rock people. Speak. Do you have answers for me?"

"Hee, hee." A small laugh comes from the orange stone. "We have given you many answers."

I take a big, deep breath and focus on the feather as it sways right and left, up and down. From the circle of stones a line begins to move out, away from the circle.

"Step on me. Follow me," the line beckons.

I am trying to figure out what the line is. Is it stones? Is it more lessons? Rock people, maybe? As I step on the line, it twinkles and shimmers. It seems as if I am walking on gold. It is a narrow line. I feel as if I have to balance. As I walk on it, it begins to change. Each step is a memory. I step forward on the memories and look behind me, to the lessons that are teachings.

In front of me are memories to come. Confusion. No, I shake my head, not confusion. A line. More than that—steps—*intentional* steps. I look to each side and there is vastness there—nothing exists on either side.

"Do not dismiss absence as nothing," says the blue stone. "Absence is always something. Go deeper than that. Grasp what is there."

"Too hard, it's too hard," I think. "I'll stay on the line and follow it across. That's right. I'm going somewhere.

"Somewhere," I keep thinking. "Somewhere."

Before me is a large stone.

"Step inside," the rock says. "Step inside and grasp the spirit."

I move towards the large rock and the next thing I know I am inside it. Around me is twinkling glitter, shimmering color, points of light, warm and inviting. The walls are crystalline, red and yellow, peach, green, orange, sky blue, purple. Shimmering light, spiralling mist. Water runs, soft and peaceful. A gentle wind blows through the chambers. I have entered the cave of spirit. It is heavy and still, a place unique. I take a step and I float. I can even fly. I rise to the top and look into the crystalline depths of power—going beyond what we know as rock—into a liquid matter, into ancientness.

"Gathered together here is spirit," I hear. "Understand that out there is not what counts. What counts is within. You have followed the line and gone deep within yourself, into the mystery school. Lessons and memories have carried you to your spirit. The shimmering has invited you home, within yourself. Here you find comfort and are ageless and boundless. You seek the sun and have found the shimmer.

"In earth terms, the sun is a simple object. It supplies light, from which comes food, that all may live. The son of the two-legged is a little one that grows into a man, who carries the name of the family. The son is a carrying-on in physical form of the spirit. Do you understand?"

A coolness surrounds me. A feeling of being dead a million years and at the same time of being alive forever. I feel water running through me, past me.

"Drink from me, eternal life, the sun," I hear. "Pull from me vastness. Hear my inner core give you your existence."

I drink from the water and feel my body become one with its softness. I am cool. I feel peace deep within my soul. I rest within this depth. Around me the light becomes very yellow with hues of orange. Suddenly I feel a flashing blast of heat, burning up, doing away with. Cracking sounds are all around me.

"What is happening here?" I ask.

"A changing. You have come for the sun. The spirit of soul is at hand. The ancientness of all spirit is the sun. The giving of life. The ebb and flow of all that is."

I can't breathe. The heat overcomes me, and then a quietness. Rich and vibrant red surrounds me. Heat like I have never known.

"I'm going to melt," I think. My oneness is all I know.

I look back to the feather, hanging there on the pole. Spirit has overcome me with the intensity of sun, the life-giving force. Then I hear a baby, the sounds of crying. A rejoicing and a sadness, all in one.

I breathe in and out. Before me I see an elder, a wise one with piercing black eyes. Lines around his eyes are like a road map: ages and ages, places and knowledge have been experienced by this elder. I am overwhelmed by the ancient map of his face. I see oriental, black, Irish, German. I see Native American. I see the tribesman, the one who moves with the land.

His ebony eyes twinkle. His hair is white and pulled back in a braid. He

Rainbow Medicine

wears a red bandana. His skin is kissed with browns and reds. His eldership is dearly earned. He is a shaman, one of great individuality, a gentleman of doing. He speaks, this elder named Sun Man.

"You have come to me on the path of the sun. You have come looking for the knowledge of your spirit. I am your guide, one who is familiar to you. All who come to the spirit world find in their guides something familiar. We of the spirit world wait here, listening for those who need assistance. We listen for your call. When you have set your intentions, made your prayers and have reached into the spirit world, we come to you. We help to steady you. We are ones who know the way—guides, elders, teachers of spirit."

His clothes are simply made and garnished with medicine. His shirt is of mixed skins—deer and elk, horse and rabbit, wolf and coyote, fox and mountain lion. Around his waist he wears a belt that catches my eye. Braided with different colors, it is made of grass, skin, cloth and wire. It is woven and knotted, and from it hang talons, hoofs, paws and tails, teeth and ears, metal objects, rock people with holes and sea creatures, including a crab. It fascinates me, this belt. I take a deep breath as the belt speaks.

"I belong to Sun Man; he has earned me. I hold the medicine he has walked. I know the ways of the prairie, the lessons of those who follow the buffalo. I know the dances in honor of the hoofed ones. I hold the medicine of the elk, the energy of mating, the drawing close, the stamina to win no matter what, the need for cleverness and wisdom, the tremendous power of the elk that Sun Man has studied. I have within me wire from fences where Sun Man has gone beyond and understood the need of the moment marked by the fence. I have within me the colors of yellow, of red and green, blue and white."

I look into the eyes of Sun Man. He speaks. "A student you are, seeking your vision. A young one, merely 19. You have listened and feel much pain. You have experienced bones that have broken, a heart that has broken. You have felt the earth and all its ugliness and know much for 19. You have come to your elders and asked to learn. You are respectful of the two-legged elder; you have listened to the teachings of respect. But your anger is great and from this comes a need to balance. You have been given a great gift."

Light shimmers in his hair, reflecting a rainbow of soft colors in his long braid. He loosens his hair, shakes his head and holds it cocked to the right. He cuts his eyes towards me and says, "It's time. I am a grandfather elder, an ancient elder of spirit, a sun guide—one who has gone through and beyond the energy, one who has listened and holds great wisdom. In your earth walk, you're a young one. I'll give to you the teachings of the sun. I'll explain to you a way that you will hold dear in your heart. Let your grandness of spirit now recall."

An intense golden glittering immerses me. I draw a deep, long breath and feel a memory of gold light—so bright it changes to white, a flash of color, small points of light everywhere.

"This is good," Sun Man says. "You have seen and now recall. Each step you take upon the path provides a point from which you can draw upon the energy of the Great Mystery."

Sun Man's eyes change to a vibrant yellow with streaks of black, a look I can never forget. "Your vision of the sun must now be revealed."

On the ground he draws a circle. On the right-hand side he draws four lines. On the bottom he draws four lines. On the left side he draws four lines. On the top he draws four lines.

He points to the four lines on the right. "This is your place of spirit. Recall." He touches the four lines and they change to red. "Confidence. It will take confidence to understand. You'll be called to have a tremendous amount of strength. Nurturing and compassion will come. Absolute is what is so."

The four lines shimmer in red. He moves to the bottom and touches the next four lines. They change to green. "Growth is so, you are growing. Beauty lies ahead of you, magic, the call of the night. Changes must be remembered and brought forth. Perfection will be at hand, just the way it is. Everything, just the way it is."

Sun Man extends a long, crooked finger and points his talking stick at the next set of lines. They glisten blue as the sky, deep as the ocean. "Within is your truth. No healings come from without. From the transformation of healing comes proof, a clarity to set you on your path."

His hand moves to the top of the circle where four white lines glisten. "The mental realm. Wisdom obtained with grand impeccability. The understanding of an elder."

He cocks his head, smiles, steps to the center of the circle and disappears. The circle becomes yellow. I hear the wind echoing in the pines, the needle singing in the high breeze. And in that song, his words: "Recall. Recall and walk through the sun."

I Hear the Rapid Beat of the Drum Calling Me Back.

The Sacred Circle and the Medicine Wheel

There are circles in your life that are needed to obtain knowledge. In contemporary shamanism there is the medicine wheel and the sacred circle. Both are sacred and both assist you in obtaining knowledge. They differ only in the fact that the medicine wheel is a circle made of stones, one stone at a time laid next to the other, each one representing a different principle and lesson.

Each medicine wheel has a flow set by the shaman that laid the wheel. There is no one way of laying a wheel: different nations, tribes and nationalities have different traditions.

The sacred circle is a place of safety for drawing power and energy. It can be made of stones or sticks; it can be drawn in the ground as a dirt circle, made of rock salt or cornmeal, outlined with different precious stones. Or it may be made of feathers or skin to encompass the power of the animal you're working with, or the lessons of the transitional tool placed in it. This is your choice.

The medicine wheel and sacred circle are places where addiction, abuse, obsession and compulsive activities may be studied as lessons. All things are welcome in a sacred circle or medicine wheel, with the understanding that they are lessons and actions to be studied and learned from.

Setting Up a Medicine Wheel

Needed: *Rocks, skulls or crystals; cornmeal and tobacco*

1. **Choosing the spot.** When building a medicine wheel, you are building a sacred circle, a place where you go for spiritual strength and discipline. The place you choose can be plain dirt or grass. One of the best locations is beside water—a pond, lake, river, ocean. The area you choose should be large enough to accommodate the number of people you want to have share your wheel. A personal wheel is 4 feet (1.2m) in diameter; a family wheel is 8 feet (2.4m) in diameter; a community wheel is 16 feet (4.8m) in diameter. You'd need the large wheel for a wedding.

   The area above the wheel should be clear and open to the sky with no branches or limbs covering it. The wheel should have an open and clear path to Great Spirit.

2. **Preparing the spot.** When you set up a wheel, you need to collect rocks that have a special meaning to you. They all must be clean and free of negative energy. No anger or discord is to be connected to the place or the rocks chosen to build the wheel.

The ground is to be clean and raked. The grass should be healthy.

3. **Starting the ceremony.** First, honor the ground with a gift of corn-meal and tobacco. Offer prayers for the coming of the spirits, for all the spirits that will come to your wheel. Remember, whom you call will come. Only ask for what you want.

4. **Placing the stones.** Place your first stone in the center to honor Great Spirit. This can be a rock, a crystal, a skull, a candle or a bowl of water. All of these are accepted symbols of Great Spirit.

   The remaining stones can be whatever you need for your cere-mony. The wheel has stones placed in a circle, starting clockwise from the east and going all the way around. There can be a rock for each subject to be worked on.

   You may also set a larger stone for each of the four directions and work with the Blue and Red crossroads. The Red Road runs from east to west and is the spirit road, the road of spirit lessons. The Blue Road runs from north to south. This is the physical road, the line of lessons learned from the physical mind and emotions. You would place a stone along these roads for each lesson you wish to learn.

5. **Types of wheels.** When you build a wheel it is important to have a teacher to guide you, for you need to honor the people you study from. Rocks are used in one kind of wheel. But there are many different traditions in Native American practice. So advice from a shaman or medicine teacher is very important for honor and respect to medicine wheel beliefs.

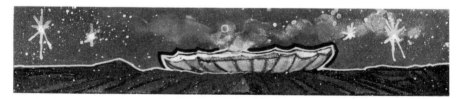

How to Find the Sacred Circle

Creating a sacred circle assists you in opening to the higher self and beginning to understand the depth of your vision. This circle is a school, a church, a home, a place of refuge.

From this sacred space, you draw energy, come to your balance point and receive creativity—the ability to organize and connect to a solid memory of times when you felt strong and enriched. It is a place that speaks to you of your medicine.

It is necessary to locate your sacred circle in a private area where it will be respected by all people. There can be more than one on your property—inside as well as outside your home. It is a very sacred site.

Recommended for an Outdoor Sacred Circle

Sacred circles often occur naturally—a ring of trees, a clear spot on a hillside, a grassy space surrounded by hedges. Any or all of the following characteristics will add to the energy of your chosen site:

1. **Open sky above the circle.** This allows you to connect with the sky, to connect with a grandfather spirit, the sun. Here you will be able to rejoice, to pray, and to do your sacred breathing and exercise routines, which open you to a higher self, as the sky is open above you.

2. **Surrounded by trees or greenery.** When seeking a sacred circle site, you may come across a group of trees or bushes that have naturally grown in a circle. If you don't, and you're working with an open piece of ground, you may wish to plant a circle of greenery. You may plant hedges, rose bushes, trees and bushes of your choice that will provide safety and security while they stand above you as a counsel of teachers.

3. **The top of a hill.** Land that is higher than the ground around it allows you to be closer to grandfather sun as well as giving you the sensation of being lofty. It also offers you the chance to climb a hill, and the opportunity to rejoice in achieving the top.

4. **A circle of energy.** This could be strong, green grass that grows in a circle. You will notice the circle of energy by the different colors of the grass, from the healthiest green to the least healthy brown. It could be the feeling of water moving in a circular motion underground, which you can sense by holding your hand above the ground and feeling. It could be a beautiful circle of flowers. It could also be earth that is rich and fertile. Find a circle of energy and build your sacred circle around it.

Preparing a Sacred Circle

1. **Outlining your objective.** I teach that it is a good thing to outline the sacred teachings of your sacred site before beginning to build the circle. Have what you wish to accomplish within the circle understood and record your intentions in your journal.

A sacred circle is a place to listen to the teachings of the Great Mystery. Bring in the keepers of wisdom by placing words into your sacred site. You may choose what you wish to learn by choosing certain words. For example, in our lodge we think of Creator in the Center; spirit in the East; emotions in the South; body, or physical, in the west; and mind, or mental, in the North. Draw upon the keepers of wisdom by placing words upon each object or direction making up your circle, going as deeply or as simply as you choose.

2. **Preparing yourself and your tools.** While building a sacred circle, it is essential that you have no negative energy. Cleanse yourself before you enter the circle space: rest, take a wash, rinse yourself with warm to moderately cool water, and relax.

Follow this by playing your drum or the ceremonial instrument of your choice, or listening to the flute or other instrumental music. Being in a good way is important while setting the energy of your circle.

Begin the construction with the ceremony of smudging, cleansing yourself and all the materials and tools you will be using. Formally and ceremonially, ask permission of the Mother that you may use the space you have chosen. Give tobacco or cornmeal or both as an expression of thanks.

3. **Focusing.** Understand that the center of the sacred circle always represents Creator energy. You may choose an item to represent and bring to focus the Great Mystery: a fire pit, a candle, a buffalo skull, a bowl of water.

Know that the four directions make four wedges of a pie that fit together and complete a circle. We mark our directions with colored flags: red in the east symbolizing confidence; green in the south symbolizing growth; blue in the west symbolizing truth; and white in the north symbolizing wisdom. To find the colors and the teachings for your circle, sit facing each direction, beginning with the east, and ask the spirits of that direction to give you a color with a word.

You may choose to build gateways in the four directions using the poles tied with the colored flags that have come to you. This sets an actual opening for you and spirits to come in and out.

4. **Energizing.** You may choose to rock the perimeter of your circle, or place poles from which twine is strung to enclose the area. We use this method, stringing the twine three to four feet (1m–1.2m) high. This provides a feeling of safety without being too closed in. Both of these techniques send energy in a spiral pattern within the sacred space.

Using a Sacred Circle

1. **Smudging, giving away.** Remember that a sacred circle must be used with respect and in a good way. Before entering, partake of the smudging ceremony. Feel the earth and the presence of the four-legged, the winged ones, the finned, the creepy crawlies, all of our relations.

   Periodically, cleanse your circle by smudging. Feed the sacred circle grounds by giving away to the four-legged, the winged ones and all our other relations. Use tobacco, cornmeal or seeds. Give away to your wheel, that all that come to it give away to you—this is the sacred circle.

2. **Moving and receiving lessons.** As you enter the circle, move in a sunwise way, always circling to the left if you are facing the center. Each time I enter, I honor the beginning and the end as one spot. I accept that I am standing on an adventure, and as I move around the wheel it speaks to me of the teachings that I bring to myself.

   Remember to respect others around you and be in a quiet, sacred way to share in the joy within any sacred circle. There should be no discordant energy or arguments in the sacred circle. Never allow children or animals to run carelessly and irresponsibly through the site. Alcohol and drugs have no place within any sacred sites.

   Here are the teachings of the Great Mystery, lessons are learned here. Receive them with respect and understanding. You may choose to write these lessons in a journal and put them in a handout to share.

   The circle is an open place, a 24-hours-a-day, seven-days a week place that energy comes into and goes out of. Come here to be blessed and draw on energy that is constantly moving in a physical and spiritual way. Even if you are 100 miles away, you can still connect in a very real way to your sacred site, drawing on the ever-present energy of Creator.

3. **Ceremonies and teaching.** The sacred circle is a place to hold ceremonies such as marriages, adoptions, bonding of family units and blessings of children. In our lodge, we also have the teachings of the sacred medicine pipe, face-paintings and name-givings. Sacred circles are places of respect and power that can be passed on to your children and the generations to come.

   Personal ceremonies are also carried out in sacred sites. I always visualize the sun and the moon, the sacred circles of truth that I know. I give thanks to Mother Earth, for she is a sacred circle. I think of the parts of myself, my spirit, my emotions, body and mind—the sacred circle that I am. To the four elements—fire, earth, water and air—I give thanks for all that is. I use my drum within this space, sitting with the teachings of my teachers, my ancestors, my elders, drawing strength from the knowledge that has been given to me.

4. **Leaving the circle.** When exiting the circle, give thanks for what has happened within this sacred space. Acknowledge your disconnection from the spirits and walk on in a clockwise direction in celebration of the sun's rising, circling and setting.

I ask you and all that you are to see the sacred circle as the energy of respect. Ask yourself if you are flowing in a circular way. Understand that each choice you make, each line you take, connected, is a circle from beginning to end and that there is no beginning and no end. Here, too, you have the sacred circle.

Aho.

· 4 ·

The East

I stand looking out. Before me the sun cracks the dark. I walk towards the sun and stand listening to the winged ones sing their morning song. I breathe in a deep breath, and let it go. The sun rises and the morning colors greet my face. I'm standing in the east.

From the woods comes a beautiful young deer, fresh, quick, gentle. It stops and greets me. I see the keenness in its young eyes. A path invites me. I walk up a rising slope in the morning light, the soft oranges, reds and yellows. The sun glistens on the green trees. The sky is blue and full of morning as the last shades of purple from the night disappear. I come to a place in the woods where it is quiet and very respectful, very sacred. Within the forest is a sanctuary, a place that houses the sacred.

As the morning sun shimmers through the pines, I see a wise one, a spirit, walking towards me, an eagle feather in its hand. The feather is spotted. From its tip comes the power of blue light, an intense call for learning, a beckoning from the Great Spirit to listen. The spirit is that of an eagle with the form of a two-legged—eyes of an eagle, face of a slender-bodied woman.

"I am Spirit Eagle," she says. "I wish to teach you. I have come as an awakening for your spirit. You have called me with your sadness. You have shown me a lack of wholeness. You have shown me a lack of understanding. Great Spirit takes form in many ways. You are given a story, a vision."

Spirit Eagle lifts her hand and points towards the sun. "From the sun to the moon, and everything in between. This is your vision. What I speak of is the medicine that you will walk with. When you go back to the earth, you have your life. You have the problems of any human. You have the doorways of growth that allow you to experience your truth. You have chosen this life and now you stand at a crossroads, coming deeper into your vision. As you understand your vision, it brings a solidity, a form, a grace and a balance that allow you to open—to have from your heart and to give from your heart.

"This feather is my give-away to earth. It comes from my body and floats to the ground. The tiny four-legged use it to build nests. The bug people live within it and build a whole city. Everything in life is a circle related at each point. When you begin to understand that this comes from that, you begin moving, flowing through the many places of time in which we have choices. As two-leggeds, Great Spirit gives you an adventure to experience. Within the space of spirit you will recall what is yours, what is given to you.

"When the two-legged dominate the earth walk, when tradition is gone, as it is, when family has gone to argument, then there will be a loss of medicine. You have been called from your spirit to hold this vision and to give it to those who wish to learn. Give them flight and allow them to soar—fly to the sun, and beyond."

I look into the sky as Spirit Eagle points, and I see the sun with rings of color around it—sunbow. I see the pastels, the pale pinks to the pale lavenders, extending from the sun. The motion of circling, spiralling towards the sun, through the sun, and beyond into energy. Vast, white, energy.

"Yes, that great white light is the Great What Is. It is the Great Mystery. And today, to you, there is no mystery that is unknown. Look there, in the white light and see the Great What Is. Draw from the spirit of recall, from the core of your spirit, and remember."

I feel myself pulling away, not wanting to remember, not wanting to think about what is happening. I want to go back to my human existence and have my chaos and problems and lock myself up with the feeling of lack, with no desire to be part of. But a swift energy, like a deer moving

Rainbow Medicine

gracefully in the woods, pulls me to the point and allows my spirit to fly.

I am pulled into the light. There, within the light, is everything—the spirit of all—from simplicity to grandness and beyond. A song, the same four verses, chant and spiral in my mind. Drums beat, the wind beckons, the fire crackles. Intensity builds. Then I feel a misty, cool refreshment that blows life in my face. It engulfs my mind, and I remember.

The spiralling motion of white light spins into reds and oranges, yellows and greens, blues and purples and burgundies. All of it in its paleness and brightness is with me—beauty like nothing I have ever seen. Gratitude rushes through me, impeccability follows. Floating in color, I begin to see form. From each pale color comes a clan of animals. From the red comes the deer, from the orange the mountain lion, from the pale yellow a hawk, from the soft green a coyote, from the blue a bear, from the purple a fox, from the burgundy a wolf. They form a circle, a council. For a moment they look like humans; they wear the regalia—beads, moccasins and feathers; they carry drums, talking sticks, coup sticks. Then they transform into animals of the forest—squirrels and mice, the raven.

In the mist of color and animals appears an elder, a two-legged with soft blue eyes. Spirit Eagle has taken on another form. He looks into my gaze and says, "This pale one is the one with eyes of the sky."

I look back into his eyes and in them I see children singing. I see elders working, planting gardens, harvesting their flowers, making bread. Life. Family. Tables with people eating together and sharing laughter.

"Pale One, show me. Show me the ways."

He turns and walks towards the sun, motioning for me to follow. I go deeper into the color. Mist engulfs me as I follow him. I know that I follow a warrior that you just conjure and go. I follow the Rainbow Warrior.

Before me all is a soft pale green mist. Swirls of color mix in, soft peach, yellow, blue and lavender. I find myself sitting beside a mountain brook with a huge waterfall behind me. I sense the Rainbow Warrior standing close, listening.

His voice calls out to me, "You have chosen to follow. You have chosen to teach. Listen for the teachings of the Seven Sacred Stars. The wolf is your inner heart—your spirit's mind. You have within you the ability to recall energy as it transforms into matter. You have the way to organize all that is and bring it forth as your path. Your ability is to comprehend and explain.

"I need you to walk the brook. You will pass through the fog. The mist will surround you and you will step into the brook. When this happens, you will connect with seven large stones. In these stones you will find the process of understanding. You will be taken to the word—to the wisdom— that you seek from each star in your vision."

It is still early morning and I hear the birds chirping. The freshness of the smells enriches me, the earth and the pines. Rainbow Warrior asks me to stand now and walk into the mist. I smell fresh mint and lemon. As I step into the mist I see a clear rushing brook in front of me. On the other side of the brook I see the Warrior's eyes, deep with knowledge, beckoning me. He wades into the brook and disappears downstream. As he leaves, I hear his closing words, "On each stone is your medicine.

"The vision of your sacred stars lies ahead of you. Honor and celebrate the teachings of each stone."

I step solidly on the first stone. Below my foot is a large, red jasper mixed with bloodstone. Intriguing. I am holding my weight balanced on one foot. As I stand there I hear a soft sound, like bells tinkling. The rock speaks.

"You seek the red star. It is the medicine of confidence. Listen and you will find your confidence."

I step to the next rock—an orange carnelian. Its words are like air; they float, each one of them, through my mind. "The orange star you seek. It is balance. Up and down. Back and forth. Here and there. Balance. Go on."

I step to the next stone, a rich yellow topaz. "You seek the yellow star, which is creativity. Go on."

I step to the green stone, a mixture of emerald, malachite and aventurine, pale to rich vibrant green. "You seek the green star. There will be growth. Go on."

I step to the next stone. I stand there, feeling the large rock of blue lapis beneath my feet. The brook rushes past me and the mist lifts as the sun breaks through the pines. The rock speaks. "You seek out the blue star, the teachings of the truth. Go on."

I step to the next rock. It is amethyst, flat and smooth, with points of purple. "You stand on the purple stone," it says, "and seek the purple star. With it are the teachings of wisdom. Go on."

I step to the burgundy stone. It is a dark, deep garnet. Through the middle runs a streak of tourmaline. "You stand on the rock of burgundy seeking the burgundy star. It is the star of impeccability."

I look ahead of me in the stream. Pieces of crystal glisten in the water like ice. "Go on. Walk the colors," I am told.

I step on the crystal and jump to the bank.

In front of me is a circle of smaller rocks, seven of them. They look the same as those I have just stepped on. "Place these in your medicine pouch and keep the teachings with you," I hear. "Walk with confidence in your vision. Balance with your vision. Be creative and grow. Know the truth in wisdom, which brings you into impeccability—the wholeness of your spirit and your physical being."

I Hear the Rapid Beat of the Drum Calling Me Back.

How to Select a Medicine Blanket

Comfort is very important to all of us, and a medicine blanket is one of the ways comfort is achieved. It is also a tool to provide safety. The blanket can be store bought. It should have many colors, or a special color or colors, but no pictures. If you choose to make it, it needs to be a full-size blanket made from 100% cotton, for the energy is pure in cotton and positive ions can flow through easily. You can hand-sew, weave or crochet it. The colors of the blanket need to be your favorite colors.

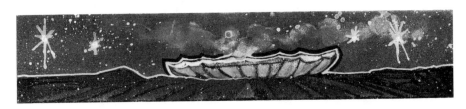

Opening to Your Spirit

1. **Find a place of comfort,** a place that is safe to you, where you have a comfortable feeling, a place where you are welcome and know that your ways are received, where you won't be hassled, betrayed or defeated before you get started.
2. **Breathe.** Take a gentle breath in through your nose, and out through your mouth. Do this four times. As you do, let go and relax.
3. **The path.** Let your eyes softly close. Begin to see a path in front of you, a familiar, comfortable and safe path.
4. **Seeing your spirit.** Begin to see mist of different colors, a soft fog of colors around you. In that space of mist and fog you'll begin to see a form. This will be your spirit. Remember that your spirit can take on many forms to teach your lessons. You can see yourself as a wolf, an elephant, a rosebush, a bee, a human, or as a spirit of light. From these forms you will find the knowledge of who you are and what you are.

There are many good books on the market now that have definitions of animals, flowers and trees, of essences, herbs and oils. My teachings are about color, so it is important to pay attention to the different colors that you see.

- To see the shades of red is to see the shades of confidence, strength, absolute and nurture.
- To see the shades of orange is to see the shades of balance, success, correct and choice.
- To see the shades of yellow is to see the shades of creativity, vision, ceremony and the ideal.
- To see the shades of green is to see the shades of growth, faith, beauty, perfection and change.
- To see the shades of blue is to see the shades of truth, understanding, healing, transformation, introspection, depth, sincerity, clarity and proof.
- To see the shades of purple is to see the shades of wisdom, power, enrichment, knowing, realness, purity and abundance.
- To see the shades of burgundy is to see the shades of impeccability, intense clarity, mystery and grandeur.

The different colors will speak to you. You may interpret them from the words that I've shared. This is the way to open to your spirit.

Smudge before you start. Journal each time you go. Each time you see and follow the path, journal the experiences that have come to you from your spirit. In this way you may begin to know the teachings that are coming to you and be able to experience the fullness and wholeness of your life.

Aho.

Rainbow Medicine

· 5 ·

The South

Before me I see four green lines. I take a deep breath in and I relax. I see these four green lines standing as stick figures. One of them is a baby coyote, the next is a youth coyote, then an adult coyote, and the last one is aged, a very old coyote. The old one watches the others dance around the baby coyote, sniffing, jumping and pawing. The adult stops and looks me in the eye.

"Why are you in our space, two-legged? What do we have that you want?" He sniffs, raises his upper lip and growls at me.

The older coyote looks sad and says, "Don't come for us. It's not our time. Sit and listen to the value of our life and you won't take it away."

"Shhh. It's okay, Grandfather," says the youth coyote. "Maybe this two-legged has not come for our pelts. Maybe it's not after our teeth or our tails."

"Mind your business, youth," the adult replies. "Grandfather Whistling Wind did not get his name by not knowing the two-legged. To me he has given the name Dancing Rain. And to you, the name Young Eyes. The baby one he has named Soft Breeze. These names carry stories of knowledge. Young Eyes, you have not seen the two-legged that call us wild and crazy. They say we steal their chickens. They say we kill and ravage, and get into garbage. They don't know. They only say, and then they shoot. This is a two-legged.

"Why have you come? Answer. Answer us why you are in our space. We have asked the question."

"I am here," I reply, "to learn the ways of the south, the desert, the summer. I am here to know why you fear us so."

"Sit, two-legged," Grandfather says.

I laugh. Grandfather is a funny coyote. He has a red bandana tied around his head. Young Eyes builds a fire for Grandfather and me. The little baby goes to sleep, curled up by his father's feet.

"Okay, two-legged. I'll tell the story of the coyote people. I'll speak to you in ways that will make you understand the life bearers. This is what we are—the story-tellers, the dancers. We're the ones who know. We have invited you to sit with us because you have come. You have crossed through the gate of the east and you have walked our way in the spring. Now you are here in the summer and you are listening to an elder of growth.

"First I was innocent: I was a baby. I learned to yip. Things have changed since then. It was wide-open spaces for me. There were very few traps and there were places that we could hide. There were not so many roads and these four-wheels that go by. There are stories of us being called the Tricksters. But we're more than that. I grew into a Young Eye, then I became an adult. You know, it's a funny thing, how the two-legged and us, we don't get along. We sing songs to you in the night. These songs, they speak of the beauty that lies around us in the earth. We sing songs to the Mother. We dance around the fire. We stay in the shadows."

I notice that as the grandfather speaks, a shadow moves between him and the adult. I catch a glimpse of red eyes and a snarling mouth with long teeth.

"Who is that? One of your cousins that stands in the shadow back there, with the red eyes?"

"Shhh," Grandfather says. "Do not speak of Red Eyes. Do not speak of the one who stands in the southwest. Shhh.

"That is the Trickster. That is where the legends come from. These are the things that get us killed. This is the one that steals the chickens. This is the one that is to blame for the sorcery."

"Sorcery?" I ask.

"Yes. The southwest is known for sorcery. It takes a rap because of sorcery."

Grandfather snarls and raises his lip. "Do not speak to Red Eyes. Do not call him into your circle unless you're willing to live with the one teaching that you will remember to have been a mistake. You'll have to live with the word mistake."

"I have no fear of Red Eyes," I say.

"No, you do not understand. You are not one of us. You are not of the south. You two-leggeds, you do not remember the spirit of yourself. You do not know who you are, do you?

"Scat. Scat. Get out of here. Sssst. Get out of here," Grandfather says to Red Eyes. "Go on. Get. Get. You are not here. Go into the shadows and stay."

Young Eyes looks at Grandfather with a questioning look. "Why is it, Grandfather, that we do not speak of Red Eyes and we do not know of the shadow? Why don't we want to know about what is there?"

Grandfather replies, "I've told you the stories of the Trickster. The southwest is full of trickery and full of stories of the Trickster. The Native two-legged pay respect to those things. They know the ways—the tests of the Trickster."

Then Grandfather looks at me. He rolls his eyes. I feel myself getting dizzy, sleepy. My eyes seem to drift off and close. When I open them, a very wise old man is sitting before me. He is a strong man, a big man. His scraggly hair is pulled back from his pitted, narrow face. His two eyeteeth seem to protrude from his lip. He wears a red bandana.

I look at him more closely and realize his hands and feet are paws and he is sitting on a tail. Hmmm . . . a coyote man.

He snarls, and says, "You're right. I am King Coyote. The lessons of the south, you are to learn. You will need your faith. Do you know it? Do you understand your growth? Do you have your faith?"

He wears a scroungy beard and mustache. And dark glasses. His eyes are covered. Oh, man! A chill runs through my body.

"What is it about you I don't like?"

"Heh, heh, heh, heh," he laughs. It is a low-pitched, evil sound. Then he gnarls and says, "Your self-persecution is why you don't like me. What's the problem? Is it fear?"

My stomach turns. I am dizzy and tired. His presence is very annoying. I turn to leave and there is a solid rock wall behind me.

He laughs.

Shadows dance around me—all over the wall. I feel fear building inside me and I begin to crawl up the wall. My fingernails slide down the surface.

"Where do you want to go now?" he asks. "Where can you go that King Coyote is not there? Why don't you change into your true form, and face me? Have you not known your vision well enough to know where you sit in the wheel? Show me your form. I want your tail. I listened to your tale. Which is it, tail? Or tale?"

"What tail?"

"I have many tales," he says. "A storyteller, I am. I could sit and talk all night, if you would listen. But you don't want to listen. You shut down. You shut down to me, and you don't listen."

I feel very tired. I know not to turn to run again, because there would just be the rock wall.

"Heh, heh, heh, heh," King Coyote laughs. "Turn around and look. Too scared? A scary tale, that's who you are. A scaredy-tail."

"I don't know this stuff about a tale. I don't know what you're talking about."

"Well, I thought you were following your vision here. I thought that you were beginning to get a grasp of what is going on. Following your tale, aren't you?"

Poof! He disappears—and I am face to face with a black cat and a white cat. Red eyes and green eyes. The green eyes of the white cat and the red eyes of the black cat. They snarl and claw and hiss at each other. They fight around me. I hear voices from the outside speaking.

"I don't know if she's going to live or not."

My mother's voice: "She has to live. She's my only child. She will live."

"If this fever doesn't break before long, she'll be going on."

"No. She's my only little girl. She'll live," my mother says.

The cats rage with meowing and hissing and snarls. They bat at each other and claw at me until the black cat engulfs me and I am inside of it. Then they fight again. Around and around and the black cat engulfs the white one. I feel the depth and the void within the mind of the cat.

"Get it right," the cat thinks. "Movement of the mind is who I am and what I am. And now, you are me. Sleek and shadowy, willowy and independent. Aloof."

The cat hunkers down and is very quiet. Secretive. It waits for the mouse that scurries in front of it. The mouse stops, waits and watches. Its small heart beats rapidly. We pounce and devour the mouse.

At that moment, the cat turns, hisses and stands eye to eye with a huge white wolf. The white wolf pounces on the black cat and devours it and I become the center of the white wolf. The wolf leaps, from the south to the north, and disappears into the night.

I stand in the center with the pole and the eagle feather. I glance back to the south and there are the four green lines.

I hear, "The tale. What is your tale?"

"The tale of the Wolf," I reply, and give out a low groan that grows into a howl. I hear that sound within my soul. I sing it forth from my spirit.

I stand in the center, looking at the south, feeling the warmth of the sun, the summer, the knowledge from the vision. My innocence is growing and I am holding to the beauty that I have seen in the white wolf I have become. The change circles me. It is perfect, just the way it is, I think.

I take a soft breath in through my nose and let it out through my mouth. I open my eyes and there is grey around me, an eerie, cold feeling. I feel doubt, then anger, then disgust. Fear rages through my body and I relax. I know I'm not alone. I recall the breaking of bones, the blood in my mouth. Danger surrounds me. I hear the clicking sound of a gun being cocked. I look to the right. There is nothing. I look to the left. There is nothing.

Memories flood my mind—not knowing which way to turn, I grasp each moment and hold solid to my vision. Then fear overcomes me. The path narrows and I walk quickly, hurrying, trying to find what is here for me to see. Emotions flood my mind. I must be—as the two-legged say—breaking down, losing my head, losing my mind.

A wicked laugh comes from among the trees. I see a small dense fire flickering there. Laughter echoes around me. Circling me, small fire spirits dance and shriek and shrill. They run to the woods, taunting, "Follow us, fearful. Follow us, fearful."

I take a deep breath and walk within the trees.

"We are your mistakes," the tree people say. "We are your inadequacies," the bushes speak. "We are your weakness; we are your emptiness; we are your disconnectedness," the water sings as it flows by. I see a fire circle and there once more is King Coyote. Around him are cages. I see red eyes in them.

"What do you have in those cages?"

"Always asking questions," he says. "I didn't bring you here for questions. I brought you here to teach you how to unlock your emotions. Otherwise, I'll keep you paralyzed here, as mine, in these cages, as the weak ones that walked in this camp before you.

"So, you're going to take on your vision and walk a life of impeccability. You want your heritage—to know your magic and your medicine. You want to heal and transform. What a foolish mistake for a small wolf!"

I feel my jaws clenching, intensity in my eyes. I breathe in through my nose, set my jaws and close my teeth together with a wolf breath of NO! It echoes through my mind.

I can hear these teachings in my mind.

"Breathe out. Set your jaws and say NO as you breathe out."

Quickly I breathe in and set my jaws.

"Don't look him in the eye." That is easy because King Coyote has sunglasses on, but at that very second he removes them. My eyes lock with his. He has a scar at the corner of his eye where his fur has been ripped away.

"If you can straighten out your emotions and stay focused on the path," he says, "you may have the right to call yourself impeccable. Look at the fools in these cages. Each one of them is trapped by its emotions, weakened by its own fear. So you feel your confidence is ahead of you. You should have it in your heart."

"I have learned so much from the sun. I have learned from my visions. I know not to look you in the eye, King Coyote! Not to weaken myself but to stay focused on my prayer, which is to follow Grandfather's vision, to seek out the beauty that lies within it and tell the stories to those who come and sit around the fire. I choose not to weaken myself and throw my life away for a mundane existence in a cage."

He turns his head sideways and snarls, "But you would lock us in a cage. You would as soon see us all there. You cannot set things in order. You have no power of impeccability. You have no tail of the wolf, only weakness. Because you walk as a two-legged you're doomed and marked to fall."

"I wish not to watch you, or listen to you any more, King Coyote. You're saddened by your own disgust and weakened by your own anger. I follow my vision no matter how hard, no matter what the cost. I'll keep my eyes firmly on my path and not bend from that, for I know the stories are within the stars."

As I speak, I feel myself tingle inside. I feel an orange flame like fire run up and down my back. I feel a solidness of red in my legs. Words of yellow flow from my mouth. My heart beats in greenness, the growth is exciting. It is fun to face King Coyote with truth and see that when blame is placed outside yourself, it weakens you.

The wisdom of my vision shows me how to free those who were caged in their emotions. It takes walking your talk. As I turn to leave, the doors of the cages spring open. With their own confidence those in the cages leap and run. Joyful laughter spreads through the woods as they disappear, leaping and bounding and running.

I turn to look at the coyote one more time.

"Ah, ah, ah. Don't look back," he says." You'll stay if you do, for I own your heart. I have given you my heart—therefore, I own yours. Because you are entangled. I'll be around again."

He licks his lips and moves around me in a slithering dance like a snake. "Do you ever think you'll get loose from your emotions?" It begins to snow, and it is hot. He laughs. "You have a lot to learn, little wolf. You have a lot to learn about mystery. And about sorcery." Two nails point at me. Two nails and his paw point back at him. "Mystery is your path. You cannot live as though you have it all figured out, for like snowfalls in the summer, so are your emotions unpredictable."

I Hear the Rapid Beat of the Drum Calling Me Back.

Making a Sticks and Stones Bundle—A Balance Bundle

Needed: *6 sticks or twigs 3–4 inches (7.5–10cm) long; 6 small rocks, one of each color; a piece of skin (deer, elk or any animal skin) or a piece of 100% red cotton, about 7 inches (17.5cm) square.*

When you have gathered your six sticks, take each one and put the thought of an emotion in it. For example, one for anger, one for sadness, one for joy, one for fear, one for acceptance, one for disgust.

Place a medicine word on each stone: Red—confidence; orange—balance; yellow—creativity; blue—truth; purple—wisdom.

When you are ready to let go of a fear, name it, break the appropriate stick in half and let go of the emotion. Then bury the two halves of the stick in the ground. Forgive and forget. Then choose one of the medicine stones and place it on the red cloth or skin. As you let go of each fear, add a medicine stone to your bundle. The bundle will have six stones in it when you are done, one for each emotion or each problem you have.

Fold the bundle by matching up the corners, top and bottom, right and left. Fold the right corner in, then the left. Then bring the bottom corner up and roll it up to the top.

You can place the bundle in your pocket or medicine bag and carry it with you to remind you that you have balanced your fears with Wisdom or Confidence or any of the colors.

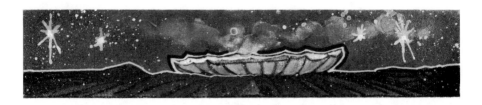

Balancing the Emotions

In balancing the emotions, we connect the knowledge of our existence to the life-giving source of the energy of the south. We must relate to the trickery of the south in order to understand our human condition. Recognize that from our fear can be built a fantasy world of evil—avenues of destruction such as extreme weight gain, extreme weight loss, eating disorders, suicide attempts, alcoholism. Fantasy stories can be concocted to detach and disconnect from reality—to avoid responsibility and accountability. The path of acceptance of our reality always lies before us as human beings, but so does the path of true sorcery, which lacks Creator energy and chooses to manipulate and destroy. It is a choice that faces each of us.

The following are the steps to take to balance the emotions, to draw growth and innocence from the south and to understand that it is energy that gives us the ability to have our balanced emotions and feel acceptance.

1. **Connect, or go to the core.** This is done by acknowledging which emotion we are acting from. There are six basic human emotions:

Acceptance	Disgust	Joy
Sadness	Anger	Fear

   It is important to acknowledge your emotions by asking yourself, "What do I feel right now?" Then find one of those six words. You will bring yourself to the core.

2. **Question and learn.** Then you can direct your attention towards what that emotion is connected to. What caused you to feel it? Ask yourself every question you can think of. Work on this process by breathing, centering and going within to your spirit. Here you will find the avenue of wisdom that is necessary for you to grow.

   Tug and pull at the question until you understand what's really going on.

   Example: Anger. I feel anger. Why am I angry? What do I want to be angry about? Which is the right thing to be angry at? How does the anger happen? Where do I go with the anger? What will I get from the anger?

3. **Show gratitude.** Take emotions like disgust, anger, fear and sadness, which are known as negative, "bad" and dishonorable, and have gratitude for them. In our need to fear or be angry or sad, we often choose to move far away from the feeling of acceptance. See what is there. If I had not felt sad, I would not have gone for the walk. If I had not been on the walk, I would not have met that wonderful person. In each thing, come around to acceptance, which is the widest band of energy that we feel as humans (band of energy being the vibrational frequency within the feeling). We have the ability to accept it if we choose. It's the strongest force Creator has given us.

4. **See light in all that you do as you walk your path.** Understand that fear has a positive side; that anger has a positive side; that disgust is a positive action; that sadness is a necessary force that allows us to follow a path of adventure known as the human existence, the earth walk. When death arrives, if acceptance is at hand, then the song or story may be sung or told. Look at it as it is and draw from life's true mystery, which allows us to see the unknown in a known way. This removes the stress on our mind.

At that point our emotions become companions and the energy between the coyote in the south and the wolf in the north begins to balance as family. The cousins are getting along, playing the game, living life with a happy force.

Aho.

· 6 ·
The West

Before me is a path darkened by heavy rain clouds. Around me are the rain beings, the thunder beings and the lightning beings. The clouds are heavy and full of soft, autumn rain. I can smell it hitting the parched earth. The earth reaches up and takes each raindrop like a kiss on the cheek and drinks each one down with gratitude. I feel a presence behind me, something casting a large shadow over me. I smell a strange odor. I hear a faint sound of sniffing. I turn, but nothing is there, except some deep marks in a tree—the scratches of a bear.

The tree speaks. "Not just a bear, not any old bear. These are the marks of Blu Bear."

"Blu Bear?"

"Yes, Blu Bear. The eyes are blue," says the tree person.

"Well, if these are the marks of a bear, and I feel the presence of a bear, where is the bear?"

"Within," replies the tree person. "You'll have to go deep within and grasp understanding. Introspection is your next step on the wheel, bringing respect for yourself from within. Out flows the way of understanding. It's an arrow through your mouth, down to your heart. It's blue."

The four lines on the tree are blue. I begin to understand, I recognize the third set of four lines on the sun in the west is the blue. I go deep within myself, sitting on a log.

"It's a good place to be—going within," says the log.

Oh, it's not so bad, I think. It's very dark and still. As I feel the rain falling around me, understanding comes over me—a way of truth. I sit on the log with my legs crossed in front of me, and rest. I feel a presence and open my eyes. There sits a grandfather. An old, old grandfather.

"I'm Bear Heart," he nods. He has a round, wrinkled face. His eyes are like little black balls and around his neck he wears a necklace of bear teeth and claws. His feet are bear paws.

"May I call you Grandfather?" I say to the spirit.

"Yes, Granddaughter. Your ways show respect. I have a lesson for you. You must listen. Bear medicine is that of the innermost spirit, knowledge of the self. These are teachings that manifest materially and allow a body to exist. Now, a body isn't an easy thing to live in, and you have come to the elder ancestor spirits to learn the lessons. You're going to have to pay attention to these ways to heal this earth mother of ours.

"If you think the ways of the King Coyote are rough, then listen to the stories of the Raven. The Raven speaks of how he escorted the dark away from the rainbow, away from the place that held the light. And each day the beautiful colors came. Listen to the story of the Raven. The Morning Star, the evil one, was taken away and was put in a dark place where there were no more colors—a place of lessons, where you walk now, called Earth. Listen to the Raven. It knows."

At that moment a huge black raven lands on the shoulder of Grandfather Bear Heart. "You listen to the Raven, the medicine of the west, the teacher of magic and knowledge of the void—the keeper of the story. This Raven protects the truth. You always know when there's sacred truth around, for the Raven will be there to guide the way. The most precious stories and truths are always guarded by the Raven.

"You must come now to the place on the wheel of the adult time, and stand now with the pain. I give you this talking stick, this stick of prayer so that you'll see a vision. You'll leave from here and go with this vision. It will touch your life and open doors of truth that allow transformation and healing. Don't walk too close to the line or you'll fall. Remember your clarity. It will be your proof."

He holds out to me a small heart, made from wood. He gives it to me. Then he holds out a blue heart, made from glass, which he gives me. Then he holds out a raven feather and gives it to me. Last, he holds out a bear claw and gives it to me.

"They hold medicine," he says. "Keep them with you, deep inside. As you grow to be an adult and you listen to two-legged words, remember—I am the keeper. I hold the Raven within the west, the blue and the black—blue so dark the black is there.

"Remember to look within, to walk the wheel you are given, the circle of the sun. All that is, comes to be. Look for the vision of the talking stick, the prayer stick, and you'll know it's time, when you're an adult, to go and teach these good things. Wait for this. The time will be in autumn."

I sit on the log, feeling the rain. Leaves fall. As they float in the air, they speak.

"You have to call on the color of each leaf. Lessons lie within their colors. Remember color: it is the magic that carries you through the autumn."

On the ground I see a grand spotted eagle feather. Beside it I see the pawprint of the bear. I turn and look: there stands a large bear, sun shimmering on black hair, and within I see the blue.

"Look at the feather," the bear speaks. "In it is all that is—the ability to soar, to float, to re-connect, to come and go."

The feather stands on its own and dances. It floats high in the air, spins around and around and swirls to the ground. It lies at my feet, its tip pointing to the west.

"What you have is within. Remember the four lines of the red and seek your spirit. Remember the four lines of the green and be able to grow, to keep your innocence and understand its path. And remember the four lines of blue—to have the introspection, to go within—within lie the answers. You cross the lines and sit within the sacred circle. There you grow with grand knowledge, and you dance. For you have been on your quest.

"All that you search for in me, the Great Feather, is respect. It starts in the mind, the recordkeeper of everything that is so, the ancient keeper of knowledge. You must follow your vision of the Wolf. You must be the wolf that you are. You have the heart and mind of the Great White Wolf. Your earth walk is one that shows people the way home. Home is the combination of the color rays that allows the path to be understood—a place to rest when the day is long and weary. Home is the kinship of family in the warm afternoon. Home is the fun, the laughter, the joy of children. Home is all things that spin in all directions, in all dimensions and realms and make a complete circle of perfection. Home is the beginning and the end. Home is something. Home is everything. Home is introspection, the ability to perceive the mind, to have the opportunity to be and to express and to walk with the tradition of impeccability. It is yours. Pick me up and hold me," Great Feather says.

I reach for the feather and before me I see huge, awesome pines, beautiful clear blue skies, land that is not damaged. The elk run, the deer stand quietly, the bear is eating, the wolf calling. I see the eagle soaring high into the sun. I feel the presence of mice and chipmunks, tiny ones peeking in the woods. I hear the cry of a baby and the moan of an old person. As I hold the feather in my hands, I hear the sounds of the Great White Wolf.

I Hear the Rapid Beat of the Drum Calling Me Back.

Making a Talking Stick

A talking stick is a tool used to let people speak their feelings in a group, or it can be used to talk and listen to the Spirit Ancestors of the Spirit World.

Needed: *A long stick, 12–18 inches (30–45cm) long; animal fur, feathers, paint, ribbons, cloth, stones, etc.*

The stick can be any type of wood. An honoring should be given to the earth and the tree. You honor the earth or tree or fire or water through a gift of tobacco or cornmeal. You always place a prayer in the tobacco or cornmeal and then just put it on or beside the area where you're working. There are many customs of honoring. These are two we use.

The stick can be carved—into a horsehead, for example, or a wolfhead, eagle feather—any carving you wish. You may paint the stick with the colors and marks you need to give the stick the power you want it to have. You can use lines, curls, any designs you wish, in the colors you want. Place fur and bones from your power animals, feathers you have found and cherish. You might glue on stones, or carve a notch and place a stone in it.

A talking stick gives you the floor to speak. All people must hear you out, as well as the spirits. They must listen to you as you sit with your talking stick.

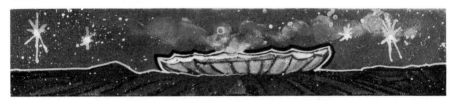

Utilizing the Physical Body

In walking the totality of your physical path, you must use introspection—the medicine of the bear—the ability to go within and be quiet in the autumn and to be prepared for the long, hard winter. This is the mystery of each day we live or the way we may die and leave this earth walk.

Our physical form has a purpose. We control it by allowing ourselves to reach deep inside our vision and to find body medicine, which is medicine of the physical plane. This medicine is known as truth, and reaching for truth, which brings the understanding of limits, is a key component in achieving wholeness of Creator energy, spirit, emotions, body and mind.

Utilizing the body consists of:

1. **Recognizing spirit in physical matter or form.** Sit with your spirit energy and draw it into complete perfection. Do this by getting a clear image of your spiritual self and its depth. Connecting your spiritual self to the physical form enables you to pursue owl medicine, the wisdom that lies within and understanding of the limitation of death. Truly know the mysteries around you by understanding that it takes dedicated energy, dedicated movement, dedicated organization and dedicated power to recognize ourselves as individual forces of matter and to consciously maintain our connection to Great Spirit.

2. **Knowing your physical limits.** In your journal, place numbers 1 through 7, followed by the physical limits listed below. Write down the facts and then explore what this means to you. How do you feel about your age, for example? Come to a place of acceptance for each fact.

1. Your age
2. Your height
3. Your weight
4. Your sex
5. Your nationality
6. The knowledge of your history through religious tradition
7. Your understanding of physical life, education of matter, physical reality

This process allows you to examine and accept what will be your shortcomings and your long comings. Expand and direct these into strengths instead of allowing them to be defeats or diminished attitudes. Through the ability to perceive and correlate, you come to an understanding of your physical body.

3. **Going to the fullest.** Organize your physical life to the fullest by taking responsibility for yourself. It is important to know about inherited physical disease as far back as four generations, to seek out the existence of diabetes, for example, heart failure, alcoholism, cancer. I recommend setting your intention at the top of the page.

   Example: My health.

Then list 1 through 25. Now brainstorm everything you know about your physical self.

   Example: High blood pressure, parent died of cardiovascular failure, parent died of diabetes, alcohol problems in parents and grandparents.

Be sure, when you're outlining the facts of your physical body, that you do not forget that the brain is a physical part. If there has been mental illness, depression or any other such problem in your family, this is not a thing to be embarrassed or ashamed about. It is necessary to understand that these are treatable, and that the mind is as much a part of the body as the heart.

3. **Listing these things.** Then you'll have the ability to seek answers and reach an understanding. This creates a very strong guide to improving the quality of your life by adapting your diet and exercise regimens to the medical history of your forebears. In this way you live a good, healthy, full life.

4. **Connecting sacred spirit to the physical and operating from a force of wholeness.** Do this by recognizing your limitations as a physical person, understanding them through the emotion of acceptance,

bringing balance into your life, and having the ability to make it physical. To physically bring forth your wholeness is to accept your limitations. You need a properly balanced diet, a properly balanced exercise program, properly balanced spiritual practices and also fun activities.

Having things to look forward to and lean back into are important parts of structuring your physical wholeness. Acknowledge your needs and how you go about meeting them. List 1 through 7—examples of what you may feel makes up your wholeness. After each one, describe what you do in your life, what actions you take, what words, what thoughts—to bring each one into fullness.

1. *Spiritual practices.* This is how you choose to interact with Great Spirit. It deals with the processes you use to rest and restore your spirit.

    Example: Yoga, prayer, music, worship

2. *Physical organization and discipline.* This is the balance of your daily life, the boundaries you use to operate within on a daily basis.

    Example: Goals, plans, exercise programs, outlines, commitment, respect for human life

3. *Ability to communicate.* This is your creativity, the way you express yourself.

    Example: Body language, your speech, your self-expression, the arts

4. *Understanding others.* The way you view others, what they mean to you, what you need from them.

    Example: Your brother and sister live away from you and you feel they should be close to you. Think about their needs, what's good for them. Think of others' needs when you combine your life with them.

5. *Recognition of Earth Mother and all the things around you that you may need. Give thanks and surrender to balance and harmony with your brothers and sisters of earth.* Understand that you are a part of everything, all of the earth, that what you do affects everyone. We are all in the web of life together.

Example: Killing of people or animals and how it affects families and balance in the animal kingdom. Understand the need for all on earth: why bugs exist, why we need clean water, fresh air and good dirt to grow food. Learn and know what destroys the earth.

6. *Ability to reach within Earth Mother and draw Grandmother energy from the moon.* This is to know the ebb and flow of all things, to feel the heartbeat of the earth. It is to study the balance of nature and understand the process of all things used in life. It is to take time to feel the soft energy of the moon, to comprehend the fullness of the moon in your life.

   Example: Earth—Understanding how we all depend on one another—that we can't live without the life of the tree people, we can't live without the water. Moon—To honor and respect the night, which is part of the flow, not a time to party and destroy life.

7. *Being in connection with Great Spirit, Grandfather/Grandmother energy.* To understand that God, Great Spirit, Creator, Father/ Mother Almighty is the same thing; that the energy of Great Spirit is not to divide but to hold together.

   Example: Prayer, and seeing all human beings as yourself, having a good place for all and knowing that all these feelings are Great Spirit. Believing we have to flow together, different as the colors in a rainbow but connected as each color within the bow.

This allows us to be on the sacred path of the grandfather spirit. To understand that our physical body is our expression of Great Spirit.

Aho.

· 7 ·

The North

I breathe in and out. I'm standing in the cold on a dark, snowy night. Around me I feel my emotions. I feel acceptance, disgust, happy, sad, anger and fear. Dancing on the snow I can actually see fear, a small purple spirit that prances in the moonlight. It stops and looks at me with piercing purple eyes that have small yellow dots in the center. It has sharp, angular features. It is inhuman. This spirit questions me.

"Do we go? Or do we stay? Could you exist without me? What would your existence be like? How would you know enough to protect yourself? All two-leggeds see me as an enemy. Please help us to share that fear is necessary. Please help us to express this to the two-legged.

"We have chosen you. We have watched you. We remember you. We have brought you here to the land of the mind and the spirit beyond so that you can remember your own knowledge of spirit life. Call forth the path and walk it each day. Take your remembrance with you and allow others to see their fears."

A scurrying sound comes from the left. I see a long, thin, straight, deep blue neon line—a tense force vibrating across the ground.

"Angerrrrrr." And it stretches on. "Angerrrrrr. We are anger. We have the ability to change good into bad. We have the energy to carry on, to push you through. Like fear, we have both sides. There is more than the negativity that two-leggeds have been taught about anger.

"The anger that you see is truth that pierces your daily walk. It's a motivation of the mind, sharp and keen. To be able to remember, you must have anger. We are part of you. We are a structuring force that allows you to prevail."

I look at the deep blue, hypnotized by the color. I feel myself inside the intense vibrational frequency. It is short and swift, pert and to the point. There is a vastness, an incredible vastness. I can hardly breathe . . .

I bounce out, back on the ground, and catch my breath. The anger dissipates and disappears.

Now I am very lonely, very sad, very lacking. The world is suddenly green—hazy and disconnected, confusing and upside down. The feeling grows stronger. It comes in waves, small and large. The green speaks.

"That's right. Sadness—it becomes your very being. Loneliness, a perception of being left. A sense of unfairness, a perception of loss. We are sadness. We can cause you to seek, to reach out, though it is not always as it seems, so bad and sad. We cause you to go beyond."

I think about sadness. I begin to vision, to feel the sun and the moon and everything in between. My vision is no longer scary. It becomes a song, dancing around me, making a circle of sacredness in my heart, my heart of hearts within the mind.

I take a deep breath and smell the four seasons. I smell it all—fruits, vegetables, the earth, rain, snow, the sun, the ocean, the mountains.

"You're happy."

A lightning bug appears, glittering and twinkling in the night. It is night and day at the same time. The winged one laughs, and each time it does the light goes on and off.

"This is joy, both light and dark," it says. "The thing you fear, the thing you are. Joy for a few moments. No worries. The ability to fly beyond and know. To know that everything will be okay. Everything is."

I can hear my heart pounding. I don't deserve this. I feel myself go deeper down, falling and rolling until I am in the dirt. It is orange sand.

"I'm not worth it." I break and run hard. I feel things cutting me, breaking my bones. I am jerked back and spun around. I feel harsh eyes peering at me, words pounding on me. Doubt. Denial. Defeat. They pound me down into the orange sand.

"I can't. I won't. I shouldn't. It's not mine. It's not right. It won't happen."

Pounding. Pounding. IT. THEY. WON'T. CAN'T. SHOULDN'T. Around me. BIG WORDS. I begin to see WORDS and they begin to SPEAK.

"You can't do anything. You're a nobody. You don't have anything. You never will. You don't know the answers."

I feel my head swelling, as if it is going to burst, like a cloud full of rain. Disgust. My mind is filled with disgust at the life we walk as two-leggeds.

"Ha, ha, ha," Disgust laughs. "And I've just begun to breathe on you. What will you do?"

I look before me. I see a tree with small red cherries. As I draw closer to it, I pass a red rose bush. I stop to look at the strength within the flower—the absoluteness. The quality that I can see in this rose is beyond any words of beauty. There are dew drops on the petals from the morning rain. I stand in total acceptance of all that is and everything that is behind me.

The cherries speak. "There is always the swiftness of life. The fast pace, the beckoning, the ups, the downs, the here's, the there's. Which is it that you choose, but most of all, what will you do?"

I stand in innocence of spirit and I accept all that is for how it is. I turn to walk the path. Before me in the grass sits a burgundy wood box. As the sun hits it, I see lines of black in the wood and an opening. I walk to the box. It has a latch, a lid to be opened. I sit down beside it. It is mysterious. Yes, it is mystery.

The box speaks and says, "You're right. In me are the greatest of all mysteries. They have been placed here by the color in which they are wrapped, burgundy. I am the mind. I am the doorway to the truth. The path home is within me. When you open me, you will have everything in your hands. You will have the ability to reach for the stars and heal the scars. The wounded will come. You will be able to go within, open me and give the path home to whose who seek."

I am overcome by the beauty of the box. I have been given Truth. I have the option to open the lid and hold the stars before me. I have the ability to dream, to vision, to complete, to endure. I reach out and touch the box.

"I am soft, don't you think?" the box whispers.

I feel the lines of the wood, the grain underneath my fingers. As I look at the box, I think of the sun. I can see shades of yellow and orange in the wood.

At that moment a bright flash of white light comes from within me out to the box. The lid flies open. I rise and feel my sharp claws, the firmness of my paws, the long fangs in my mouth—the teeth that can break bones—

my piercing, rich, burgundy-red eyes. Each hair glimmers in the silvery white sunshine and my tail is strong and powerful. I am the White Wolf.

Suddenly it is night. Standing in the frozen grass with the lid of the box open, I sense something calling me from the box. I take a breath and let it go, and it becomes wind in front of me. I feel from inside out. I know what is in the box. I know the way home. I know the path. I feel the need to run, to howl. I turn and there stands a beautiful woman, her arms extended. In her hands she holds clay and a stick. This sister, this strong sister speaks of balance. In her face I see the form of a buffalo. In honor we stand together as family. Around our feet is a circle of seven stars.

"The teachings are within the mind," the box says. "The sacredness of the path home and the life of prayer are yours, as sisters, to give to all. Your stories are eternal, as are all of those who have sat in the Council of Elders, the Wisdom, the Great What Is."

I draw from the absolute power that I feel within the howl of my own song. The call of the wild in the winter night, I remember. It is correct, ideal and perfect. I sit with the burgundy box in my hands. I stroke the open lid. I look within. There I see clarity—the pure reflection of the Great Mystery. I look across and the woman of the buffalo is in prayer, her wisdom timeless in her eyes. Her intensity is impeccable.

It seems she is looking through smoke as she says, "The truth is the arrow, the white arrow, the way. I seek that white arrow, I seek that way. I long for sacredness to be born, for respect to be allowed. From these prayers, I find you. In the cold, an elder I recognize, a sister of the animal circle, a keeper of wisdom."

She disappears. Those moments were like eternity. I look again inside the box. I see a crystal blue pond, a hawk soaring, spiralling over the pond. Diving through the water, it disappears. I run towards the pond, towards clarity. As I dive through the water, chasing the hawk, I feel a purity, an enhancement, an everlasting, eternal illumination. At that moment there is a burst of energy that explodes into color. Dots of light all around me, I spin through the swirling color, soaring. The hawk takes wing and points its way downward. Following the hawk, I too spin downwards.

I find myself on a familiar path. It is very dark. In that vast blackness, deep purple and dark blue mix together as points of light, twinkling above me. One of the spots of light catches my eye. I hear a voice.

"You're staring! Shall I come closer?"

The light in the sky approaches me, taking the form of a child star, a star with arms and legs and a little pointed head, little pointed hands, little pointed feet. It shimmers and twinkles.

"You can talk, Star," I say.

"Yes, I can. I am Talking Star. I'm the guide beyond your mind. I've come to teach you how to go beyond. Follow me."

I begin walking. I'm walking on air, stepping up out of the earth realm. I am among the stars, millions and millions of points of light.

"What are all these lights?"

"They're all beliefs," Talking Star replies. "They are beliefs of power, of truth, of creativity. They are beliefs of choices and changes, of proof and impeccability. Absolute beliefs, perfect beliefs."

They are beautiful, all the points of light. They come together and provide a path, a path of seven colors: there are red, orange, yellow, green, blue, purple and burgundy stars. Talking Star and I walk on them.

"Where are we going?"

"We're following stars. We're beyond the north, beyond imagination now. You have imagined this beautiful realm and we've stepped beyond. We're beyond fantasy. We've stepped into the path of journey and we've gone beyond to the spirit world, the upper world, where the teachers are."

Before me I see a very large, shiny object. It looks like a giant crystal.

"What is that, Talking Star? Up ahead of me," I ask.

"It is ice—but like no ice that you have ever seen. It is the gateway to the mind. It comes from where you have come."

I walk slowly towards the large crystal. When I come close, I see my reflection in it. There stands a beautiful white wolf with seeking eyes and streaks of black in its face and on its back and paws. Its nails are black. I turn my head to the left, and it turns its head to the left. I turn my head to the right, and it turns its head to the right.

"Why is it, Talking Star, when I look in the ice I see the Great White Wolf?"

Talking Star replies, "You see yourself."

I step into the ice and through it. As I walk, I see four white lines, sharp and cold. I step each step deliberately, one in front of another, as a four-legged would walk. I enter a small door—it is the door of wisdom. There I feel the strong presence of knowing. I turn and there are yellow eyes looking at me. The eyes begin to speak.

"Here is creativity, the ability to imagine. To live as a two-legged and bring forth all that is. To create life. To end life. To make something out of life."

When I look in the eyes, I feel the depth of Truth. I remember a feeling that comforts me, a feeling of family, but much, much deeper. In front of me stands the owner of the yellow eyes, a very old wolf.

"Who are you?" I ask.

"I am the keeper of ancient wisdom."

"You look so old," I say.

"I am not old, I am wise. I have come and I have seen. I have given and I have received."

The wolf walks and motions for me to follow. I go inside the white line of wisdom, I hear small tinkling sounds that are familiar. I feel myself understanding the depth of knowing. I stand with the old wolf of wisdom and look out in front of me, as the wolf points. I see millions and millions of points of light, all different colors.

"What is this? What is this beauty that I'm looking at?"

The wolf turns its head slowly and looks at me. "The other side. You're on the other side. This is how it looks to us."

I look out at the vast points of lights—at the reds, the pale oranges, the very, very pale greens to the deepest and richest green—that twinkle all around me. The feeling is overwhelming. I *know*.

The wolf motions for me to exit through the white door that I came through. I pass back through the doorway and look again at the four lines.

In the second line stands a presence, a deep, dark figure. I see its paws and nails. As I draw closer, I sense the wolf. I sense its power.

The wolf nods and looks me in the eye with deep, rich, red eyes. "I am the pathway of power. Come with me and I'll show you."

The wolf enters into the white line, which becomes a doorway. It runs, faster than anything I have ever seen. I follow on my four legs. As we pass through the doorway I feel my muscles unleash, and I run like a shooting star. What a grand and magnificent feeling to run like wind, leaping and lunging, each muscle performing in excellence. I look beside me and there is the awesome black wolf. As our nails dig in the ground, gold sparks shoot out around us.

Then the black wolf suddenly stops, and so do I. In front of us is a dark vastness. The black wolf looks at me hard with ebony eyes. Its red eyes have turned ebony black, so black they disappear into its face and the face blends into the darkness. I stand there in this presence, in this immensely black space. Yet I see a shimmer of light.

Ahead of me is the white door. I step through the line and return to the other side. I look at the third line, waiting to see who will appear. No one comes. There is only another doorway, another white line.

The line becomes inviting, pulling me in. I enter the line and step through the door. There before me stands my own reflected presence—the wolf that I have become, my familiar self. I put my hand out and there is a paw. I touch it.

"Your realness," that wolf replies, "your realness, that which you are." I wonder if it is a mirror.

"Your realness, that which I am," echoes back.

I touch my chest, feel my fur. I am real. As I watch, the wolf touches itself. It is real. I take a big, deep breath and when I let it out I hear a very strong and powerful howl. I turn, face the door and walk back.

Standing on the other side, I look at the fourth white line and a fourth door. Beyond it is a shimmering silver light, a feeling of "Come here . . ." I enter the line, step through the door and stand in the brightest white light. I can feel and hear this light. It sounds like snow and bells and wind and soft piano music. It swirls as points of light twinkle around me. Magnificent, iridescent color shimmers in the cold air.

In front of me stands an enormous silver wolf with soft dark lines outlining its deep, sky blue eyes.

"Where am I, in this fourth line?"

The wolf looks at me with a depth that runs cold inside me.

"Purity," it growls. A deep-throated, guttural sound follows the word. "You are within purity."

I feel as if I am awake and asleep, floating and standing still. Suddenly I am forced backwards in a strong rush. In front of me are the four lines. To my right is Talking Star, looking at me with curiosity.

Talking Star says, "You have entered and completed your vision of the sun. You have walked to the north, where all is known. These are your answers. Take them now, for as a two-legged you will keep your real self in your heart, which lives inside your mind. You have been given a glimpse of ancient wisdom. You have seen power and know your realness. You have stood in the presence of purity. Each point of light, each star, is here for you. Each one will answer when you call.

"You will go now. You will go now. You will go now. You will go now." The words echo through my mind.

I Hear the Rapid Beat of the Drum Calling Me Back.

Prayer Ties

Prayer ties are used in a ceremony that is done in a safe, quiet place while you are balanced and focused.

Needed: *100% cotton cloth in all seven rainbow colors; scissors; tobacco or cornmeal; white cotton string or yarn*

Prayer ties are constructed of 100% cotton cloth, torn into two-inch (5cm) squares. Keep on hand a supply of all seven colors—red, orange, yellow, green, blue, purple and burgundy—for Great Spirit may call you to work with the specific energy of one of the colors, a combination of several or all of them.

Loose-leaf tobacco or cornmeal is used to fill the prayer ties and white 100% cotton string is usually used to tie them. Cotton thread or yarn may also be used, as may string, thread or yarn of any of the seven colors. Remember, the color that you tie with imparts a specific energy, so choose from the place of knowledge and respect.

To begin the prayer tie ceremony, lay the cloth squares, tobacco or cornmeal and string in front of you. Hold the tobacco or cornmeal close to your heart, placing your prayer within it. Then put it in the center of a cloth square. Bring the edges up, making up a bundle, and wrap the string around the gathered edges, just above the bulge of the filling. Wrap three times. To set the first bundle, twist the leading edge of the string into a loop and cinch it around the first three wraps. This forms the fourth wrap and when pulled tight acts as a knot. The following prayer ties can be looped back on the trailing string and cinched tight for the fourth wrap.

As your prayer ties increase, you may wish to roll them into a ball, wrap them around a smooth stick, or lay them in a neat circle within your prayer space. You may keep adding to them over the course of days or months, or you may do a series for one ceremony only. At some point they will need to be "released." This is done by hanging them *outside* in a sacred place, or by ceremonially burning them.

Opening the Mind

1. **List in your journal all the things you don't like.** These can be things that anger you, things you're afraid of, things that disgust you, things that make you sad. They can also be positive things that make you happy but that you don't like. List them all.

2. **Core these things.** Coring is done by first going to the very beginning and understanding why you feel the way you do. Is it greed or selfishness? Is it persecution? Is it envy? Is it a lack of relationship? Is it

a lack of responsibility or accountability on your part or someone else's? Then key off certain words.

Example: I'm very angry with my job situation.

Core this by keying off the words "job situation." What do they mean to you? Where is the accountability or the responsibility? The selfishness? The persecution? You might say, "I am in a very persecuted position, because people look to me for advice. They take from my mind. It is also a very responsible position because people come to me for answers."

Accept that you have chosen to be in this position. Then identify how it serves you. What benefits are you receiving?

Example: I need to feel needed. This need is met by answering people's questions, even though I also feel used.

Identify the "even though's." Decide whether you really want to live with them.

Accept that the emotion you feel—in this case the anger—is yours, not someone else's. It's very important to understand that the process of coring allows you to open your mind and expand it beyond the small thinking of being angry.

3. **Sit with each situation that you have cored and walk a new walk.** Transform your "even though's."

Example: Instead of being angry and disenchanted with your job, expand your perception and create ways that you can help your co-workers to understand their career frustrations. Put forth examples of how you would like your job environment to be. Using these positive examples as a focus, find solutions to what isn't working.

If you have realized that you are not willing to live with the "even though's," know that you now have opened the door to new job possibilities or new situations in general, by recognizing and accepting your boundaries. Keeping those in mind, begin taking realistic and balanced steps towards finding more suitable employment.

See your emotions in balance because you are on your path, and understand that you are applying confidence, which is the ability to expand in a wide-rayed band. Accept the values that all things have and that there is good in all things.

See the limits and expectations of all. Understand both the narrowness of mind and the wisdom that are at hand. Develop the ability to go within yourself, understanding that it is hard to find the core, but that the rewards of knowing your true self are great. Be able to take your time and flow and see the good in that; this teaches patience.

See your mental capabilities and capacities. Understand your shortcomings. Are you patient or not? Are you enthused or not? Are you balanced or not? Bring this into the reality of understanding.

By recognizing and accepting what you truly need and what your boundaries are, you are being honest with yourself, and you're taking care of yourself.

By choosing to walk your true path, to "walk your talk," you remove the daily negative clutter that blocks a free-flowing relationship with Great Spirit. By choosing to be true to yourself, you open your eyes to the multitude of rich possibilities Grandfather/Grandmother provides for each of us.

4. **Open your mind to Spirit as all light—bright, illuminating and full of quality.** Allow yourself to have that light. Be all that is yours. In everything there are colors—brilliant, vibrant and soft colors that will penetrate your walk. Find them, see them, and know that they are your birthright.

   To open your mind, it is necessary to sit with yourself four times a day for at least 15 minutes. Start the morning with a balancing routine of breathing, meditation, gentle exercise and prayer. Establish your center point or balance point, where you feel most connected to Great Spirit.

   Check this point at noon, early evening and before you go to bed. Take the time to bring yourself back to your balance point. As you become skilled in breathing, meditation, prayer and gentle stretching, you will require less time to reach your center. You will also begin to "center" more frequently, quickly realizing when you are "off your path"—thus disconnected from Creator—and bringing yourself back.

   While opening your mind, you expand your path. This allows you to draw to you the fullness of your vision and to create an avenue that connects you to the flow of the Great What Is.

   When we separate from Great Spirit, we shut down. We are not open to the fullness of our mind, the gateway of our spirit, which allows us to feel heart energy. Opening our mind allows heart energy to expand, and we begin walking the way of the wolf.

Aho.

· 8 ·

The Red Star

The path I see in front of me is familiar. I recognize the red dirt and feel comfortable on it. I feel my mind and hear all my emotions, the daily life thoughts and feelings being sorted and analyzed. As I walk, the predominant feeling is sadness. Before me is a lovely tree, full of red oak leaves. As the sun strikes their beautiful red color, a leaf floats down and lands at my feet. Another moves through the air, softly floating towards me.

"Why don't you get on us and ride?" ask the leaves. "Just hop on one of us and come for a ride."

"No, I can't ride on a leaf. I'm too big," I reply.

"Oh, no. In the land of spirit, there is no such thing as too big. You can do anything that you believe you can do. That's probably your major problem, that you don't believe that you can do anything."

This strong voice comes from the tree itself. I look at the tree and see its face. It is a strong, ageless face, one with great confidence and strength.

"You can do anything. Just get on one of the leaves and ride. It would be good for you."

I want to get on the leaf but I feel fear, fear that I will fall. I also feel anger, knowing that it isn't possible to ride on a leaf from a tree. How many times I wished that I could do it?

"Come on. Come on."

Other leaves float along the path. I decide that it is possible. I jump up and land on one of the leaves in midair. The leaf bolts and jumps as if it were a wild horse bucking in a rodeo, and away we go, soaring in the sky. I sit on the back of the leaf, holding on to the edges, feeling free.

"Wow! This is great!"

"Well, when you believe you can do things, it opens up the avenue to wonderful adventures. To deny possibilities brings about defeat."

"Well, yes, but I know realistically that a two-legged can't just get on a leaf and go floating through the air like this."

I look around and there are many leaves. They are all staying in a group, swirling and turning, and we are soaring in the air together.

"Well, let us take you someplace where you meet a wise one who can explain to you why two-leggeds can't."

Our journey is long—beyond the earth, to a realm of soft mist, a place of silence and peacefulness. We float into a forest where there are many leaves in the air with two-leggeds riding and laughing. The leaf stops at a large rock beside a grove of pine trees.

"You'll see a path on the other side of the rock. Follow it to the tree people. Listen to their wisdom with your heart open and understand what is being said to you."

I step past the large rock onto the path leading into the trees. They are all pines—tall and close together, which makes it very dark. As I walk through the pines, I hear, "A tree grows in a circle, an everlasting spiral in which the energy comes from the tip of the roots and spirals up. We represent the power of living a full circle. We are ever-green, ever-growing; we are the on-going proof that life is eternal. Our greenness is a mark of grand beauty. We embody grace as the wind blows through our branches. We have within us a fortitude of faith. We are the evergreens and the pines."

I walk on to a grove of oaks. "We are the ones of strength and discipline, the ones that have the ability to see and to know, to focus and remain abundant. We are strong and produce great food. Our acorns return to the earth mother and cycle again. We are used for building, for we will last for hundreds of years. We are the strong oaks."

I notice that there are also many maples, their yellow leaves shimmering in the sun. "We represent abundance and variety. We are used for many things. We produce a substance that sweetens your world. We are the maple people."

As I walk this path through the forest, I encounter many people: the apples, which speak of love and magic and the ability to heal old wounds of memory; the mimosa, which represents romance in the fragrant spring and the beginning of the cycle; the weeping willow, which teaches bending before breaking. It has the ability to sway with the wind and teaches us to flow with all things, for there are lessons within.

The poplars speak of being straight and reaching beyond. There seems no limit to their height as they reach into the sky with answers on every twig. They are known as the answer trees. The hemlock—deadly to the touch of spirit, whose potions remove the physical form—is known as the nullifier, the one who banishes and has the strength to come up against.

There are the elms—the trees of endurance, who stand in parched ground with little water, providing safety for the bug people.

Then there are the fruit trees. The pear trees speak of creativity. They call themselves the suppliers, producing sweetness that feeds the earth.

The peach trees, which speak of feminine energy and have the gift of motherhood, have the ability to heal from their pulse and give strength to a two-legged's broken limb. The cherry trees speak of the full cycle. "We are round. We show the roundness, the energy of beginning and ending. Complete, as a circle. We are the tree of completeness."

I see many tree people laughing, sharing stories and their knowledge. They tell about how they send their energy through their roots and speak to each other. They share tales of long ago and pass on to each other the wisdom of how to keep two-legged healthy and alive.

I stand in the presence of a redwood tree, a grandfather many, many hundreds of years old. A huge tree, it stands within a grove of old growth. "We have the secrets of life in us," it says. "We give out what is necessary for a two-legged to live, through our breath. The two-leggeds breathe what we give away, and they give away so we might breathe, for we feed off of each other's exhale. It is the beginning and the end. Without the two-legged we cannot live. Without us, the two-legged cannot live. We hold the memories of giant forests, the ability to endure long and live in a strong and steady way.

"As an old growth I give you knowledge from the spirit world, that to have Mother Earth there must be a continual cycle of seeing, hearing, knowing and doing. We stand long in the forest and listen to the stories that are recorded within us. The vastness of life is what we are, and we pass that on to the next and the next."

I look up into the vast old growth, through the limbs into the sky that has darkened with night. There, through the leaves of the redwood, I see one tiny, red star glistening and twinkling. It is solid red in the black sky. It grows

Rainbow Medicine

stronger and seems to be hurtling towards me. It is. It comes faster and faster and seems to land right in front of me, but then it disappears.

I look behind me and the path has disappeared. Fear rushes in. I hear the night wind brushing through the trees behind me.

"Courage," say the oaks. "Draw on your courage."

My mind floods with the feeling of defeat. How am I going to get out of here? I feel locked away in a place from which I can never escape.

"Strength. Everlasting strength," I hear from the pine people. "You must use your ever-green, your ability to have faith and move through this. Keep walking. Follow your path."

I see no path. Fear locks my feet and I cannot move. I begin to shake and gasp for air. It is so dark, so still. Then I begin to push the feelings of fear away. I swing out and grab hold of my faith. I make a conscious choice to follow my path, no matter what, I trust in Great Spirit. I take the first step in the darkness. Then another and another, one foot in front of the other. Carefully, I walk through the solid darkness.

Before me I see a soft orange and reddish yellow light. It looks like a fire inside a house, a soft, inviting flame. Before me is a little, crooked cabin, a magical place made from twisted wood. Flames dance on the walls inside and there is a warm, comfortable feeling. As I come closer to the house, I see there are red flowers around it—red geraniums, red pansies, red petunias, red roses, red gladiolus, red snapdragons. I can smell their fragrance in the night. I take a deep breath. It is good to be among the flower people. I come to a small door. A red heart hangs on it, with the word "Welcome."

When I knock on the door, it gently opens wide. I see the fire and the fireplace inside.

"Come in," a strong voice calls. "Come in and have a sit, and let's talk about fear."

I step into this small house. I smell cherry pie baking and stewed apples. It feels so warm and so comfortable. By the fire, in a rocking chair, I see an old person. It looks like an ordinary two-legged. This old person has a blanket wrapped around its shoulders, sitting and rocking by the fire.

"Come here and sit with me. Let me talk to you about your fear, about your anger, about your disgust."

I come closer to the spirit. Its face is in shadow, its head bowed. The being points its finger at a small stool. I sit on the stool for what seems like hours. Finally the being speaks.

"Do you feel the comfort around you? Do you know your medicine when it is close to you? Are you aware when you enter the doors? Do you understand each step that you take? Do you have the ability to know your earth walk beneath your feet? Do you have the wisdom to understand where you are?"

The being seems to be male, a very old, old man with strong hands.

"Yes. I have done much with these hands."

The being reads my mind.

"Yes. I have used these hands to do many things, to prepare many things, to bring about many things, to cause many things."

"Who are you?" I ask.

The being looks at me. There are red stars in its eyes, the same that I saw in the sky. The red stars twinkle and vibrate, pulsing with a vibrant depth of color. I become lost in the ruby red eyes.

"Who am I? I am confidence. Grandfather confidence. The energy of the first."

With that, the door blows shut and slams harshly. There is a swirling sensation and all around the room red lights come on—candles flame up in deep red glasses. Redness is all around us. The color is brilliant and pulsating.

"I am confidence, the ability to have. Without me, fear will overcome you. I have called you to my home to share with you the secrets of the beginning, the teachings that you will walk with, that will provide lessons for many.

"Confidence has within it the knowing, the ability to plan, to start the process. I am the first grandfather of the Rainbow Path, the Red Star. You will study with me and I will always be with you. We will walk this long earth walk together and I will whisper to you the confidence needed to direct the paths of forgiveness. I will whisper to you the confidence needed to complete them. When the days become long and tiresome, and the darkness slips around you, you will remember the red that calls in the night, that lightens your load, that gives you the passion to go on.

"If you lose your confidence, it will be through temptation. Temptation will summon you to give up. Many times, as you have asked to become an adult and to be a wise one, you have forgotten the richness, the color that lies before you. Never again forget the small strip of burgundy that is the absolute, correct way. Never forget the family of the wolf and the memories that you hold sacred.

"You are on your path, walking your vision, and it has brought you to me to learn lessons. I will be woven in and out of your existence into eternity. Unless you choose to reject me, to give up your confidence and to forget who I am."

I am mesmerized by the twinkling eyes.

"You are in a spirit land, on a shamanic journey. You have gone within the realm of the mind, where the answers are. Learning from us, your ancestor spirits, will give you the ability to perceive all that is necessary to have your vision."

"Grandfather, my earth walk is difficult. Since I was a small child I have seen the sun and the stars and the moon. I am now at an age when I must start to walk. I do not know my direction. It's that time when one chooses what to be as a two-legged."

Grandfather Red Star laughs. "You do not choose what you are going to be, you become what you are. This is why you are in my home, listening to confidence—to know what is so for you. You are a voice, one who speaks. You were born in the time of the stars that allows you to speak. You have been given the words and your confidence allows them to flow.

"It will be your job to teach those who ask questions, to nurture them with the answers that come from within themselves. You are placed on the Earth Mother to show your walk. You have the ability to give away. The give away of red requires that you go forth in your human life and find the tokens that give you the confidence to become what you are."

"Grandfather, when I'm there on earth, working, will I be able to hear your guidance? May I come to your warm home and listen to your words?"

Grandfather Red Star's eyes twinkle. "You will gaze into the heavens and see my eyes. You will close your eyes and see mine. Remember that you are real, for this is confidence. Remember that you have the ability to go beyond and have what you seek. You are a teacher of life. Listen to your heart, for it is the center of your mind. It is the balance point where you listen to Great Spirit, which speaks through the ancestor teachers. Listen to your vision and the stars will speak to you of the seven medicines—the gateway to all."

Grandfather Red Star extends his hand. In it is a tiny red stone that looks like a ball, smooth and round.

"Here, I want you to hold this stone in your spirit hand."

I take the stone.

"Now hold it to your heart and honor it as your self medicine. Pull it within your heart."

As I pull the stone close to my heart, Grandfather begins to chant. He hums; to and fro the sound goes.

"Hold it next to your heart, Granddaughter, and breathe in and out. Continue breathing softly and remember who you are. That is the value of existence that allows each moment to happen. As long as there are moments, there is the need to know. Now place the small stone in your spirit heart and feel your confidence."

I put the red stone inside my heart.

"Your heart is red, the clay of our people, the way of confidence. Each time your heart beats, its pounding will be solid and you will draw strength from it. You will have the ability to reach out, beyond. Each time your heart beats, it beats of red. It pulsates with confidence. There is no need for fear or anger. There must be the awakening and the adjustment, then the fullness. You will see this as you walk your earth walk, and others will learn from you. Now, sit in my rocking chair and rest awhile."

I do as Grandfather says and feel the comfort of his red medicine blanket wrapped warmly around me. My eyes grow heavy. When I awake, Grandfather is watching me. I look in his powerful eyes and see the brightness of the red twinkling stars.

"Grandfather, I have come to do my disciplines and to learn techniques, to walk the path and master confidence."

"Ah," he replies. "Good, Granddaughter. I will give you the test of confidence. You will listen, you will watch and you will know what confidence is."

The old spirit waves his hands in front of him, back and forth. The more he waves them, the more I am able to see. He is making something appear by moving his hands. All of a sudden, a deep hole opens up in the floor in front of him, and in it are snakes. The hole is large enough so that I could get into it. I find myself thinking about being in the hole with the snakes.

"Step into the hole, child. Know your confidence. Show me what your confidence is."

I slip off the edge of the side, and jump down to the center. There around me are seven rattlesnakes, coiled and hissing, baring their fangs. Seven rattles vibrate. I feel fear from the bottom of my feet to the top of my head.

He says, "Now breathe in through your nose. Breathe in and out and steady yourself. Breathe in and feel your eyes begin to see as a snake would see. Breathe in, watch the snakes and move as they would move."

I begin to move slowly, in a slithering motion, in my mind. I am at peace, a deep feeling of peace. I relinquish fear somewhere inside of my breathing. I begin to hiss. I feel my slithery, pointed tongue. My eyes move like a snake's. I feel very, very cold. In that coldness is a solidity.

I look around at my brother and sister snake people. They too are at peace, their fangs at rest. Their little tongues dart in and out and there is no noise of rattles.

"Now, Granddaughter, step through them, to the other side of the hole, and come out where I am."

I feel a total connection to the earth as I move one foot in front of the other, but my body moves as a snake's would—to and fro—past my brother and sister snakes. I step into the space where Grandfather Red Star stands.

Rainbow Medicine

His eyes glisten, and in them is a vastness, a stillness, a solidity that I can feel. He puts his hands out in fists, and moves them in a waving motion in front of him, up above his head, then down.

"To you."

He points his fists at me and I move mine in a waving motion above my head. As they come down, I feel confidence, patience, acceptance—an intense self-love—an ability to be aware.

I sit down on the stool and look back at the pit where the snakes had been. They are gone. On the floor beneath Grandfather Red Star's feet there is dense, cloudy red smoke. He blinks his star eyes, and the vapors disappear.

"Grandfather, what is this movement?" I ask. "What have we done?"

He turns his head to me and slowly stares with his pointed face. "It is the acceptance of confidence, the transformation from fear to completeness. You will now recall the totality of patience, the ability to weave, the ability to tell.

"Granddaughter, it is good to teach you the lessons of Great Spirit, Grandfather and Grandmother Creator. In the snake dance, confidence was your movement. You were connected to Great Spirit and you did not make a false step. You did not make a wrong move. What is it similar to?"

"Grandfather, it is the way of life. Sometimes one wrong move and you're dead. When I lose confidence is when I make a wrong move. When I move from fear, I take a step off my path. Life seems so unfair."

"Granddaughter, listen to the wind tonight. There you will hear the song of patience. Each breeze blows a teaching. With each breath you take, draw in confidence, peacefulness, endurance."

I look at Grandfather. He holds an object in each hand. "Now, the test of confidence is here. In one hand is the end, in the other is the walk. It is yours now, Granddaughter," he says, "to know which one is so for you. Your time has come to choose—the end or the walk."

I look at Grandfather Red Star and think, "If I were to walk into the medicine wheel, which way would I step first? It would be to the left, so I will take your right hand." He opens it and in his hand is a deer hoof.

"You have chosen the walk, Granddaughter, the track of the deer. A gift to you of the medicine within the deer hoof, the medicine of confidence, of gentleness, of fair play, of soft ways."

I look at the hoof and see a beautiful fawn in the morning light. I watch it leap with joy. I feel this in my heart, a knowing that is rich and full. A peaceful gentleness is upon me as I take the deer hoof in my hand.

"Put it in your heart, and keep it with your stone, Granddaughter. It is the medicine of red."

I take a deep breath and the hoof becomes a part of my heart. I place the memory of the deer's gentleness, its soft eyes, its loving look, in my mind.

"Yes, Granddaughter. Now take these medicines and give them to those who ask on your walk. It is confidence that is the first stone, the doorway, the opening. Confidence is the beginning.

"Go back now, to your two-legged world, and gather your tokens of confidence. Organize them and teach them. Remember to look into my eyes. When the fear of the dark is on the back of your neck, look to my eyes and remember the confidence that beats within your heart."

I Hear the Rapid Beat of the Drum Calling Me Back.

Shell Rattle

Needed: *2 clam shells; hot glue gun; glue stick; paints; small rocks;*
crystals; peas; rice; BBs.

Take one clam shell and place small rocks, peas, rice or BBs in it. Next, place thoughts of confidence in the shell, or in the pieces that you place in the shell—this is your medicine. Then glue the two halves of the shell together to make one shell rattle. Paint the outside of the rattle with any symbols you choose. You now have a hand-sized rattle that is easy to carry with you.

Use the rattle by shaking it and listening to your thoughts while rattling. Remember that this is to help you feel safe, centered and full. It will build your confidence and balance you. The sound of the rattle raises your energy.

Rainbow Medicine

The Journey of Confidence

1. **Build a sacred cornmeal circle** (see page 43), a quiet place where you can sit, draw energy and relax. It can be inside or outside as long as it feels safe. Breathe in through your nose and out through your mouth four times and relax. Release all the stress, all the worry, and all the physical world around you.

2. **Journal.** Open your journal and write down anything that may be bothering you. Anything that you may be angry about or upset with. Anything that would keep you from accomplishing what you choose.

3. **The wise one.** Take a deep breath in through your mouth, hold it, counting to four, and let it out gently through your mouth. Continue breathing in and out. This breathing is an important part of balancing to start your journey of confidence.

   Let your eyes close. In a relaxed position, visualize your path. It is to be daylight, very bright, sunny and cheerful. As you follow this path, pay attention to everything you see. You will come to a wise one, a spirit, that represents confidence to you. Pay attention to what it says, what it does, what it shows you. Pay attention to what you learn from this spiritual connection, the gifts that you are given and where they are placed when they are given to you. Spend time with this spirit, this wise one, this being of confidence. The spirit may be in the form of an animal—four-legged or winged, crawly or swimmer. Remember, any of these are possible forms that confidence may take. Then come back to your present space.

4. **Journal** what you saw, everything that you felt, all the emotions you had. List things that give you confidence, things that show you the depth of yourself.

   You can do this confidence journey as often as you wish, connecting to your inner spirit of confidence.

5. **The inner rock circle.** Return to the path and build a circle of stones within your heart. In the center, place a stone that is red, one that connects you with confidence and Great Spirit, one that gives you a feeling of high energy, of the passion that goes with the color red.

   Each one of the stones will show you a lesson and speak to you. You'll find that these fulfill your innermost spiritual needs. Remember each rock and connect with the lessons it brings.

   Focus on your feelings in the rock circle and the strength that you obtain through confidence. Stand in your circle with the red center and honor Great Spirit Grandfather and Grandmother, feeling confidence inside you. Know that you have the ability to do all and be all.

6. **Journal.** Leave this confidence rock circle within yourself and come back to your present space. Journal the rocks, the words that were given to you, and the feelings connected to the issues you dealt with.
7. Correlate the words that you received from the rocks with objects that could become medicine.

> *Example:* One of your words for confidence might be "strength." The object that you choose could be a stone from the ocean that you gathered on a day when you felt strong, happy and connected. You would get that stone from your possessions and place it in your medicine pouch, or place it where you would look at it daily.

You may have a stone that represents swiftness—a marble that is clear, pale blue, looks like water and rolls quickly.

Continue to search out objects from your home or surroundings that match the needs, in a physical way, of the lessons of your medicine circle of confidence. Place them in your medicine pouch or within daily sight. From time to time, or when you feel you have lost your confidence, sit with those objects and remember what you have inside your heart, inside your mind, inside your spirit. Draw strength from them and you will have the confidence to journey through each day of your earth walk, experiencing everything in a good way.

8. Take a strip of red cloth two inches (5cm) wide and 14 inches (35cm) long. It should be of 100% cotton. Select a stick that is three to four feet (1–1.2m) long. Tie the red strip of cloth to the top of the stick. Put it in the ground by your front or back door, whichever one you use to leave your home each day. It will remind you, each time you leave and return, that you walk your earth walk with confidence, and that, in your medicine pouch, you have what it takes to remember the lessons of the sacred circle of confidence that is within yourself.

Remember that you have gone on your vision, the journey of confidence, and you have found the symbols of confidence within yourself. Know you have thought this through in a good way. You may stand by your stick with the red flag on it when you don't feel confident. Remember that you have the ability to accept things as they are. It is important, when looking at your confidence pole, to remember to have the confidence to accept. Acceptance is a key part in the journey of confidence.

Aho.

· 9 ·

The Orange Star

I breathe in and out very lightly. I feel myself walking on a familiar path. It takes me through the desert at sunset. I see orange and red rocks all around me, and I smell the dirt smells. In the sunset the mountains turn black. The evening sky is full of purples, burgundies and blues. I walk higher and deeper into the mountains. The evening turns to night and it becomes very dark. I feel the vastness of the desert.

I walk among the rocks and sense their strength. They speak. "Wolf. You that walks with four firm feet, come within the rock. You must find the gateway of calmness. When you have entered the gateway of calmness, there are six more gates to pass before you achieve your balance. You are on the quest of orange now. Keep looking for the gateway of calmness."

Before me lies a crooked walking stick. I pick it up. It seems to be a piece of pine or hickory—just perfect for me to walk with to steady my way along the rugged path. I go slowly along the rock wall as I enter the mountain mesas. I place the stick in front of each one of my steps as I walk into the night, looking for the gateway of calmness.

Before me a shimmering orange light bounces off the canyon wall. It seems to be a campfire. Its reflection flickers on the sides of the rock walls. I have walked my way deep into the crevices of the canyons. As I draw closer to the campfire, I see a shadowed gateway reflected on the rock walls. I feel the stillness of the night. I feel patience move swiftly through my body. This must be the gateway of calmness, I think. I look to each side and listen for a voice. There is nothing there.

I step through the gateway and take a deep breath. Before me is the campfire. I stand alone. I accept that: it is a good feeling, to be alone. One step at a time, I move closer to the fire. A strong voice comes from the wind.

"Walk clockwise around the fire and dance like the deer. There you will find the gateway to assuredness."

One step at a time I begin to prance around the fire. I feel my spirit rise with each flame. I spin up and down, knees up high. I step, I prance, I dance quickly. I hear the wind echo through my mind, "This is the gateway to assuredness. Each movement you take is mine. Now look for the gate of self-control."

My heart is pounding as I spin faster, the night wind blowing through my hair. I prance with pride, with conviction. I swing around, pause, and as I stand in the silence, I see the gateway of self-control. I can feel my heart beating in my throat. I howl into the night and the sound echoes off the canyon walls.

Assuredness has taken me to the gateway of self-control. Each fear, each doubt seems to disappear. I feel my eyes focus sharply. The longing to be in balance is mine. I laugh and continue dancing. I smell the night air all around me, and the freshness of the fall. It is a good thing. Each step takes me more into self-control. As my feet pound the dirt, ancient messages come to my mind. Voices chant and sing as I dance.

"Now," the voice calls out. "Now, the gate of rest."

I lower my head and take each step deliberately. I seem to strut around the fire, my movements slowing. The yellow-orange flames flicker on the canyon walls. Slower my steps, more deliberate my breath. My heart pounding, I take a deep breath. I watch my shadow. I breathe in deeply. I feel my lungs working strongly. Self-control is mine. Sweat drips from my forehead.

The flames grow smaller and quieter. I begin to walk, easy, easy steps around the fire. I slowly sit. I lean my arms behind me and rest back on my hands, throw my head back and feel my hair in the wind. I take a deep breath of rest. The gateway of rest. My mind is still. No trouble. No fear. I

Rainbow Medicine

look for angers that have lived there, but they are quiet. I am in acceptance. My legs are numb, my body full and rich. I rest.

Shadows begin to dance on the canyon walls, dark movements darting to and fro. Chanting and rattling, drumming and calls of the wind echo in the canyon. Mystery is around me, holding me by the shoulders. In the shadows I see a being coming towards me. Out of the dark spins a blanket, striped in many colors. A high-stepping, strutting dancer walks into the realm of the fire around me.

"Shhhh. It's rest," the spirit whispers.

I feel fear rising in my throat. I focus my eyes sharply and my lips snarl. The dancer prances around the fire, and then, coming closer, sits in front of me.

"You have gone through the gateway of rest," it says. "Together we sit in the stillness of rest, a line you stand upon between the choice of anxiety and self-control. Rest."

The spirit extends its hand. I see what looks like a cat's paw, with claws that are sharp, set into long, thin, willowy fingers. One finger reaches out and points to my chin. It moves up the side of my face and touches the corner of my eye, then pulls its razor nail down the side of my face.

"The line of balance has been marked. You are standing in my home. In the dance of the shadows the choice of evil is good, right is wrong, up is down, backward is forward."

The spirit laughs and the sound echoes through the canyon, spinning over my head. I look up. Above me are tiny orange stars twinkling in the sky. The spirit reaches into the sky with a swooshing sound and the stars fall into his hand.

"Good evening. I am Grandfather Orange Star."

With that, he casts the orange stars over my head and they twinkle down around me, bouncing on the ground and disappearing into the dirt. Except for one that he holds in his hand. He flips it up into the air and it falls onto his nose, where it remains. He has cast the blanket from around his head and before me is a strong-featured, thin-lined face, with long silverish-gold hair that shimmers in the light of the fire. Yellowish-green eyes peer at me from his dark, wrinkled face with an orange star for a nose.

"I welcome you and ask you to seek the next door. This will be the door of adjustment, a space where you spend time in the desert and adjust your fears. A place where you and I will come to a word that is strong within the energy of orange. Here I will give you the lessons, through the doorways of balance. I will teach you what brings about evil, what brings about loss.

"Peer deep within yourself, be quiet, and sit in the night. Wait. Look for the gate."

There is a clucking sound and, with a snap, the fire and the spirit disappear. I sit alone in the canyon in the dark. No light. No sound. A stillness. From the cliff high beside me, I hear what I think is a growl. I'm not alone. I sense a large animal. I listen. A hiss similar to a snake's, and then a growl. A cat. My heart begins to pound in my chest. Fear is in my face.

"I'm looking for the gateway to adjustment," I say.

Everything that I am angry about floods through my mind—each injustice I have seen, the wrongs I have known. They unbalance me. I can't move. I am frozen with disgust. Lightning breaks against the canyon walls outlining a huge cat.

I draw a deep breath. I think of the star on Grandfather Orange Star's nose, the peculiar shading of his greenish-yellow eyes, the angular lines of his face, the ancient wrinkles. How mysterious his hand is as he points towards me. I focus. At that moment, I enter the door of adjustment. I have adjusted and accepted my fears. I know the cat is large, and peering down on me. I know that if it were to give one pounce, I would belong to that cat.

A voice echoes through the canyon. "You must find the door of equivalence. Come forth and stand. Walk towards me."

I stand, and start to walk through the canyon. A wind swirls around my feet, raising and spinning the sand around me. It blows in my eyes and I see little sparks of energy; shimmering shades of gold and orange flash in front of my face.

"Come closer. The gateway of equivalence is beyond. Step towards it. Come beyond."

In front of me is a line. It seems as if the canyon ends. As I step up to the edge, I see a vast hole before me that goes down, deep down, beyond.

"Don't move," the voice calls. "Look at the vastness of the void and become equal."

I feel my being expand. The void beckons me but I hold steady. Around me spins the sand and the wind pushing from behind; the void calls from in front. I am very small and the void vast, very large. I hold on. I become very still. A surrendering feeling. The gateway of equivalence is now at hand. I feel one with the void. I let go, and all is quiet. The wind settles. I have entered the gateway of equivalence.

I feel it is time to turn and walk into the stillness of the deep night. Something swishes past me, like a bat. I remember the gateway and I adjust. A sadness comes over me, then a happiness. It seems as if one side is happy and one is sad. And then I split again, one side is angry and one side is peaceful—four quadrants: sadness, happiness, anger, peace. I stand, a point in that circle. A gold ring emerges around my feet, spinning clockwise. I stand in its goldness. The peace and the anger become one and spin into the gold circle. The happiness and the sadness become one and spin into the gold circle.

As sunrise begins, bright, orange rays expand above the mountains.

"You have entered the gate of totality. It is a circle of night and day."

I watch the sun rise in the canyon as the light hits the orange rocks around me. I look at where I had been the night before and remember the different gateways. I start to leave, using the crooked walking stick.

I feel a tapping on my shoulder. I turn and there stands Grandfather Orange Star. He holds out a golden ring.

"You have come for your vision of the orange star. Within this ring lies balance, to be entered into through the gate of being total. For you to be total there must be equivalence, the ability to be equal. Start by adjusting with rest and assuredness, self-control and calmness. In a canyon in the desert ancient wisdom awaits you. Simply call, and the ability to balance will be yours. In the fire lie the secrets of balance. Where the shadows live, wisdom is yours in one thought. Step not from the line of self-confidence, but walk in self-balance."

As I move along I feel the earth's energy. Energy itself is my thought. I wonder what we are. When we are two-legged, I wonder what we are. Why do we exist? What would be the purpose in living to die, to bring sadness to people? What would be the reason for that?

I walk higher into the spirit world. I look back to earth and there I see tears, murders, funerals, lives that cause trauma in the mind of the two-legged. What is the purpose in this? Maybe the orange stars can show me.

I walk on. I see a great many things, but no orange stars. Day goes on for a long time and night does not come. I begin to tire, to become weary. I remember the words, the gateway of rest. Beside me I see a place that seems inviting, a very large rock beside a river. I stretch out on the rock and lie very still with the sun on me. I breathe in and out. The thoughts and teachings of spirit swirl through my mind as the water swishes past me.

Suddenly, I feel uneasy, as if I am being watched, as if something is going to take my life away. Fear runs through my body. Across the water stands a woman, but she is no ordinary two-legged. She looks at me with eyes that are empty holes. She is willowy, with long dark hair that drifts in the breeze. Her eyes have an emptiness that beckons me. I feel I will disappear if I go. The sound of the water is louder.

I realize the rock is now in the center of the river. I don't understand how I got from the bank to the middle. The woman gives a disconnected, hollow laugh. I see that her hands have sharp claws and, when the sun hits her right, she looks like a black cat. Her eyes are now yellow, yet the hollowness remains. She extends her finger with the long nail, and beckons me to come closer. My eyes feel very heavy. The sound of the river comforts me as I lie on the rock and watch her. Her figure is perfect, a womanly delight. I shift my eyes away and watch the clouds float overhead. I find myself falling deep within sleep.

I wake to a twinkling sound and orange stars falling before my eyes. I am careful not to roll off the rock into the river, simply to find I am on a soft bed that has squeaky springs. I wonder where I am. There are tiny orange stars all around me on the bed. I am comfortable and warm, snuggled within a blanket of many stripes. I am in a little house, an unfamiliar place, yet with the presence of home. A small stove, a rocking chair, a table and a couple of chairs, with a cup where someone is having coffee. A fresh pitcher of orange juice sits on the table with a glass. I can hardly move, I am so tired—yet rested. It is strange being scared and comfortable, hot and cold. I pull the blanket from me, put my feet on the old wooden floor and walk to the open door. There, a ways in front of me, rushes the river.

"Yes, the river," I hear from behind me. "A place of choice. Do you, or don't you? Will you, or won't you? Can you, or can't you? Should you, or shouldn't you?"

I spin around and there stands Grandfather Orange Star. His face is strong and angular—different. His eyes are soft and an orangish brown. Orange is prominent in the markings on his face. Around his shoulders is a beautiful skin of cougar with the paws hanging down. He is dressed as a man, pants and shirt, a familiar belt with objects. As I look closer, I see they are stars.

"These are the lessons that you have come to learn at the river."

I feel weak. I sit at the table and pour a glass of orange juice.

"I guess I'm in the spirit world, because things are so unique here. This vision is getting to me. I can't tell what is real."

Grandfather Orange Star throws back his head and bolts out a laugh. From his mouth come tiny gold and orange stars that glitter and bounce around me. Each one of them laughs and dances on the table. I hear songs around me.

"Haven't you learned yet that there is no division between spirit and the physical? Don't you understand that it's just the line of balance?"

He removes his belt, places it on the table and sits. His hands are old and weathered. His eyes seem welcoming and unwelcoming at the same time.

"If you don't get it right, you'll fall," he says. "You've got to grasp some words and get them clear within your mind. I am here to explain to you how clarity became confusion. I want you to balance. I want you to understand good and bad at the same time. Divide the bad from the good, and there is nothing. There is no challenge. There is no defeat. Keep steady as you go and you'll understand the motivation of evil. You'll understand the balance of justice.

"I remember when Grandfather Spirit, creator of all, was speaking in the beginning," he says. "I remember when He was talking about self-control. The conversation went something like . . ."

I broke in, "I remember that conversation. I can see it. It is about self-confidence. We are to organize. Our purpose is to stay organized to create creativity. And everything would exist. There would be a perfect balance and a need for all."

"Yes," says Grandfather Orange Star, shaking his head. "You're beginning to balance now. You're beginning to remember."

"I do," I reply. "I remember the calm. I remember the bright, white light and coming from it seven colors."

"Yes," says Grandfather. "Speak more of this, Wolf."

"I remember seven main spirits. I remember the beginning, the walk. One must start at confidence. Confidence is the necessity."

I am having a hard time pulling my memories out of my mind. A soft orange mist swirls, engulfing me. There is a feeling of coolness in the mist, an assuredness. I remember what poise and trust are.

"That's it! It is trust, right, Grandfather?"

"Right," Grandfather Orange Star replies. "In the beginning Creator gave courage and backbone, strong faith, a sense of security. There is trust."

Then I feel things shift. I feel a wave, a shake. Everything seems to teeter and rock.

Grandfather Orange Star laughs, and says, "Now, it's balance."

There is a settling. Choice is at hand. There is this way or that. A measure. The ability to balance.

"That's right, Granddaughter Wolf. This ability is always present. The clarity to know the confusion of denying."

An energy soars within me. A choice is mine. If I don't like it, I can leave.

There is a swirling mist of green energy outlined by orange.

"We the orange and green spirits of energy instruct you to understand rebellion. The movement of temptation allows one to resist—to turn away in defiance and rejection, to be non-compliant, to refuse allegiance. With no path beneath the feet, one can be simply rebellious, defying or resisting established authority—making the choice to stand against.

"It is yours, Granddaughter Wolf, to allow those who listen to the medicine to restore the memory of flowing together. To understand the healing of control and tradition. To have an ability to set the movement of acceptance in motion."

The energy of green and orange spin around and dissipate in coolness and calmness. I stand once again in the ring of nine colors. Each color becomes a star and the silver and gold become a soft energy above and below. I am standing in the hand of Grandfather Orange Star.

"Granddaughter Wolf, do you understand the choice to renounce and denounce? It has brought about a tradition of spirit that is empty and absent. It is nothingness, the loss of mind, the dilly-dally, the lack of self-control. In truth, you will see the need to understand in order to to commit. In truth, you will find reverence.

"No more can one stand out of control. For in balance is a sober state of understanding, awake and totally called."

I return to my seat at the table. Then Grandfather Orange Star shifts into cat form before my eyes. His cougar robe is now his hands. Then he shifts back to an old man with weathered hands and long fingers. He places seven orange stars on the table. "The seventh one, granddaughter, is yours. It is necessary for you to keep this orange star. You must understand the need to guard, rule and order. Not to deal pain, not to push away, but to set total understanding. To find where is the lie. When evenness and stability are broken, when common sense is lost, each individual needs the orange star of balance. When it seems as if the mind is drifting away and broken into pieces—at the turning point, at the crisis, at the critical point—it is the time to step into balance."

Grandfather Orange Star places the seventh orange star in my left hand and has me make a fist around it. He tells me to hold it ungarnished, undecorated, unsheltered and naked.

"Remember to keep it smooth," he says. "Hold it in your mind. There you will have the ability to be open, outright and clear. It will be a necessary medicine for you."

I Hear the Rapid Beat of the Drum Calling Me Back.

Rainbow Medicine

The Balance Walk

Needed: *Dirt or sandy earth with no grass; cornmeal or tobacco; a stick for drawing a line; 2 sticks 3–4 feet (9–1.2m) tall for prayer poles; a piece of string 60 feet long in a color of your choice; 2-inch-wide strip of red cotton cloth*

Select a quiet spot in the sand or in the dirt where there is no grass; you can remove the grass yourself, if necessary. The area should be about four feet (1.2m) wide by 40 feet (12m) long. This area will become a balance area.

First, honor the area by placing cornmeal or tobacco on the earth. Then, with a stick, draw a straight line 40 feet (12m) long on the ground. Go on to intersect the line with seven additional lines four feet (1.2m) long.

The first area is Confidence, the next Balance, the next Creativity, next Growth, next Truth, next Wisdom and the last area is Impeccability.

When your drawing is complete, place one prayer pole, with the red cotton cloth tied around the top, at the beginning of the line, but 4 feet (1.2m) away from it.

Tie the string to the prayer pole. And now, facing the 40-foot line, pull the string to the end of the line. There you place the second prayer pole, tying the string to it. You now have a "clothesline" for prayer ties.

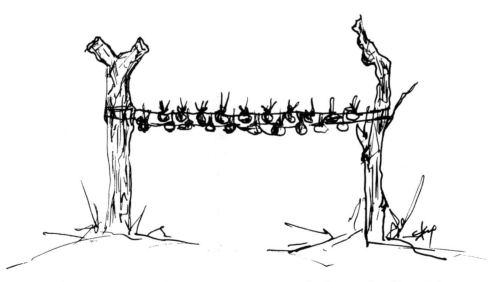

When you wish to obtain balance, come to the line and walk it. When you wobble or fall, you can read what medicine you need by what area you are in. To gain balance, tie 100 prayer ties (page 74–75) of the appropriate color, and hang them on the prayer line. This will give balance to any matter.

The colors, of course, are:

Confidence:	red	Truth:	blue
Balance:	orange	Wisdom:	purple
Creativity:	yellow	Impeccability:	burgundy
Growth:	green		

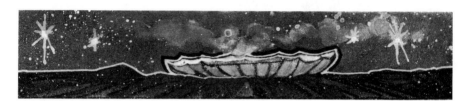

The Teachings and Process of Balance

1. **Build a cornmeal circle** (page 15). Give tobacco to the earth in respect of the spirits around you. Place yourself in the circle in a relaxed position. Have your medicine blanket with you for comfort. The blanket will shield you from energy shifts that may weaken or cause temperature changes in your body or physical environment.
2. **Take out your journal** and ask yourself the following questions:
    1. What are the things that unbalance me?
    2. What am I like when I am unbalanced?
    3. Whose fault is the imbalance?
    4. What is the core of fault?

    Finding the answers to these questions is done by careful thinking. To gain your balance, it is necessary to find the faults.

    - First, breathe in and out and relax. Let your eyes close.
    - Begin to see an image, an image that is connected to self-confidence.

        Example: When I think of self-confidence, I see a strong oak tree.

    - Keep that image in your mind's eye and bring it back to reality by journalling it.
    - Do this for the four acts of balance:
        1. Self-confidence
        2. Self-assuredness
        3. Self-control
        4. Self-esteem

Rainbow Medicine

- When you have recorded all four symbols, journal them and come to understand what they are.

    Example: The large oak tree represents my stamina in being a writer and a contemporary shaman. In my self-confidence there are changes that go through the seasons of everyday life. This is the act of application of spiritual balance to the physical existence.

3. While sitting in the cornmeal circle, **visualize your needs in life**. These would be dreams, goals and plans.

    Example: Education, marriage, owning land, etc.

Then make a Short-Term Goals Outline that will cover all the steps that need to be taken to achieve that dream, goal or plan. This could be a plan for one day—or it could span the rest of your life.

Total balance—setting goals

- Set the purpose of your life. Write your goals in order. Remember, they are subject to change!
- Know the intention. You have the sky to reach for in life. Your dreams are intentions. Write them and draw paths from them.
- Set the goals. It is good to list all feelings of intention.

    Example: Education (kind); achieving the education; using the education to . . .

Have and see the outcome. Having a daily reminder to see the purpose and goals you set keeps you centered.

See

- Have a calmness. Be in a restful mode and relax. Visualize things the way you want them to be and write them down. Whatever the subject may be, see the outcome the way you need it to be.
- Outline the steps above to bring them into realization.

    Example: 1. My purpose is to improve certain relationships.
    2. I will need to work on them every day.

- See yourself with assurance, not with anger, as motivation. To do this, you first need to accept things as they are. Assuredness comes from understanding that all things are from the Creator and that they move in a good way.

Follow these seven steps to achieve balance:

1. **Breathe and relax.** Deep breathing sets a flow. Breathe in through the nose and out through the mouth four times. Establish a breathing cycle, in which you are calm and centered in your thoughts. Relax. The word "sober" is at hand. This is not to be done under the influence of a hallucinogen, drugs or alcohol.

   Relax and become aligned with the word balance. Realize that there is bad and good, right and wrong.

2. **Organize.** Write down your strengths and weaknesses. Be honest with yourself. It is important to get your strengths in order so that you have the ability to succeed. This enables you to change avenues or alter the structure of your path through confidence.

3. **Set goals.** Line out short- and long-term goals.

   Example: The short-term goal of honoring the four directions gives me the ability to reach the long-term goal of walking a spiritual path.

4. **Take the action involved**—the actual doing. Write what you will do each day to achieve your goals. With balance comes the ability to do, to walk surefooted on the earth. To be a sober two-legged in balance is a good walk.

5. **Get the proof.** Know that you will be able to see your efforts in the process of balance come back to you in an achieved goal. That will be your proof. Later, when you recognize that this has happened, record your success in your journal.

6. **Get the wisdom,** which is the outcome. You'll be able to see things as they truly are—the mistakes as well as the achievements that are at hand. As in number 5, write in your journal what you have learned.

7. **Celebrate.** It's important to remember to celebrate and tell yourself that you've done a good job when receiving results from the process of balance.

When you have completed these steps and feel as if you have the situation under control, take a few moments in your cornmeal circle to pay attention to the world around you. Look at the things that make you feel good, and the things that make you feel bad. Understand that it takes both in order to feel.

Aho.

· 10 ·
The Yellow Star

Before me I see a familiar path. I become an eagle and I fly high, following the path. I circle and soar higher, towards the sun. I soar above the water, spiral and turn. As I land, my talons transform into the paws of a coyote. I run along the edge of a lake that stretches for miles. I sniff and search for food.

I come upon a dark cave and I enter. I feel myself becoming fierce and strong, as I take up the walk of a bear. My claws rip into the ground. I feel my large bones, strong teeth, a snarl.

I see the full moon ahead. I howl and know my wolf sounds, each hair and the bushy tail. I have circled the sun. I realize this as the sun peers above the mountains. I have gone deep within on the path. I am sitting in the early morning light watching the sunrise.

A mouse stands in front of me. "Why are you here? What is it that you seek, wolf person?"

I rattle my mind, emptying each word into the mouse's hands. "I've come to follow the path. I'm looking for Grandfather Yellow Star. I'm excited to find the next star."

The mouse hops up on a tiny little stick, sits with its little leg crossed, and looks at me. "Would you know Yellow Star? Do you know who you're looking for? Do you have the ability to know?"

"Well, of course." I think for a second. I have my orange star, the balancing memory. "Yes, mouse, I would know who I'm looking for. I'm looking for a spirit who will probably have a blanket. Part of its body will be yellow stars. I can hardly wait."

"Shhh," the little mouse interrupts. "I don't think you'd know if you saw the yellow star. You see, I know the teachings of the yellow star. I have the answers you're looking for."

The mouse scurries off ahead of me on the path. I follow, the yellow energy of morning around me. The mouse challenges me with its stamina. The morning grows to noon; the sun grows yellow and bright. The color is dry and strong.

Before me lie two yellow feathers. I pick them up.

"Yellow feathers, there must be a yellow bird. At least I'm close, the colors are here. I'm on the right path."

Before me I see an array of yellow stones. Moonstones, light topaz and yellow rocks of sulfur—all yellow stones blending together and forming a yellow path. The mouse scurries across and disappears into the weeds beside the path. I am walking on the yellow stones, waiting for them to speak.

A fox, which seems to have just appeared on the path, says, "I have come to teach you the lessons of creativity. I am from the path and I am clever. You must be clever to find Grandfather Yellow Star."

"So I am on the right path."

"Yes, but you'll need to adapt to the lessons. It will take more than just being talented. As you walk the earth walk, you are dipped in the bucket of creativity, the ability of making. You'll need more than to be skilled, to adapt here."

We walk along, the fox and I, while it speaks to me of lessons. Something in the grass on my right catches my eye. The mouse, maybe. My eyes dart to the right, then back to the path, and to the left, to the fox, which has disappeared. Before me, far away, is a dot in the sky—soaring and circling, drifting, coming closer. Above me is a hawk. *Pssssss.* The sound of the hawk echoes in the wind, as it floats above me. The spiralling of the hawk is impeccable, perfect, each wing spread so gracefully. The hawk dives towards me, soars past and lands in a tree next to me. I see its yellow eyes.

Rainbow Medicine

Then the hawk jumps to the ground and becomes a marvelous man. I feel the magic in his yellow eyes, now darkened. I am inspired by the look of his face.

"Come quick, and follow me. You are on the path of the yellow star, the making, the creativity."

"Who are you?" I ask.

"I am Hawk, the messenger. I am the mark of the artist, the craftsman, the producer. I bring the message of ideal circumstances. I bring to you establishment and motivation. The ability to perceive an ideal."

As we walk, I sense the young hawk man aging. His hair whitens, his eyes are rimmed with yellow. We come to a forest where there are trees of all types and shapes.

"You must choose," he says. "You must find the tree person of creativity who will reveal to you the story of the yellow star."

A strong wind engulfs me. It removes the hawk creature from my presence. As he leaves, his feet become talons that cling to the air, and his wings lift him high above me. He disappears in the powerful wind. Before me are the trees.

"Which one is the tree of creativity?" I call out. "Which one of you? Answer."

The trees laugh. Their voices are familiar. It seems as if each laugh has its own color. I am beginning to recognize things in shades, deeper for purple, heavier for red. I see aspens, their yellow leaves shimmering. I walk into the grove of aspens and their presence envelops me. I sit among the golden yellows in the center of the aspen grove. I am first happy, and then sad.

"You seek the word to be artist and author. You seek the knowledge of your vision, a visionary you are. You have chosen the grove of aspens due to the yellow shimmers, the sunlight catching on their leaves that enhances your vision. You are able to see ceremony and bring forth the teachings of Rainbow Medicine. We honor you and respect you."

Through the trees I think I see the hawk land and walk down the path towards me. A familiar old spirit, he enriches me with each step. As he walks closer, I notice that there are seven cloth bags, one of each color, hanging from his belt. His hands are pale and withered, his fingers long and narrow. Long, yellowish white hair flows midway down his chest from his beard. A long thin mustache hangs down the sides. His eyes are deep-set and clear, in their centers yellow stars. On his earlobes are earrings of yellow stars. He wears a floppy hat made of straw. He is covered in a loose, flowing coat, from shoulders to the ground. Beneath the coat I see his long, thin toes, each nail a yellow star.

He spins around seven full times and bows. When he stands, he looks at me with his long piercing nose, his finely detailed lips.

"It is I you seek. I am Grandfather Yellow Star. The lessons of creativity will follow."

He turns precisely and steps away. I run to catch him, my heart pounding with excitement. As I catch up, he speaks.

"I have walked the earth walk and felt the imbalance. I know the loss of confidence. It is each two-legged's choice to be clear or not—to follow Grandfather Spirit, Great Spirit, or not. We walk to the edge and we listen to Great Spirit. It is our job, those of us of creativity, to be God-like, to be masters of art—where there are no rules, where there is no line. Where happy thoughts are, always. We have the ability to share with others the enthusiasm of creating."

He turns his head softly to the left, and quickly to the right. He extends his right hand and turns it palm up, rolling two fingers in, two fingers out. It is a hand I recognize. I have seen it many times in my mind. On his finger is a yellow gold band with stars.

"Let me help you," he says. "Let me show you the way to creativity. Never turn back. Step each step with grace, with imagination, with fantasy. Step beyond, into the journey, and walk into the spirit. You may choose to paint, to construct, to give. It is all ours, to be creative."

He spins his hand in the air and makes a circle. From it tiny yellow stars rain down around me. As they light on my shoulders, I hear:

"You can. You must. You will. You are."

Before me I see a rainbow path of all seven colors. It rolls over the hillsides, soft and inviting. I walk the path in my mind's eye. The animals are healthy, children play. Stories I hear, funny ones and sad ones. There is music, many songs. Thoughts become real and I am among them. Bright yellow stars spin on their points. I stand in awe of what I feel.

Before me, are seven hawk feathers. I gather them and hold them in my hand.

"You must have these hawk feathers to point your way." Grandfather Yellow Star places his hand on my left shoulder. "Hold tightly to the hawk feathers. The secrets lie hidden within. The ability to be divine, to ride the river, to walk on the wind. Before you lies the test."

I realize that I don't want to walk this path. Yet another test! Facing Grandfather Yellow Star would not be an easy thing if I fall. I take a deep breath and let it go, gently. I choose to know. I choose to understand. I begin to walk the path. I listen carefully as I walk, and I hear the discipline. It is not a choice of confusion or rejection, but one of organization. There needs to be commitment.

Before me I see a beautiful waterfall. I sit on a large rock and watch the water pound below. The water speaks to me.

"The earth has made its commitment to teach the lessons of nature. It is a simple lesson. It is hard for the two-legged to understand—eat or be eaten, kill or be killed, succeed or fail, do or don't. These lessons of balance have come now to creativity."

The water's outer edge is smooth and calm. In the center of the turbulence the water rolls.

"It isn't a choice of anger and violence. It is one of commitment. It is necessary to create," the water says. "Gaze in and understand what is on the other side."

I look in the pond, deeper and deeper within; a stillness encircles me.

"Commitment is your first task. Then discipline. Then action. Then outcome. Each step that you take is the art of your life. It is all yours to create, but commitment comes first."

As I look in the water, I see Grandfather's face. As the ripples move, eyes wriggle. The stars on his hat swing back and forth. The tiny old face in the water calls me to commitment.

"Is it your vision? Or is it someone else's? Do you quest for your vision for the wholeness of yourself, or for others?"

I listen to the waterfall pound and roll over the rocks.

"Which is it? Your calling, your vision, or another's? Follow me. Learn the dedication of your vision. Come deeper within the water. Walk behind the waterfall. There you will meet the Rainbow Warrior. There you will stand in the presence of the pathway of growth. You will be invited to find the wisdom of the green star. First you must create your commitment."

I look ahead of me at the waterfall. My commitment will be to step into the water. The intention is the waterfall, and the purpose is behind. In a flash I realize that this is no small vision, that it is my life, and my children's life. It is my niece's and nephew's, it is my brother's and sister's. It is my reality as a two-legged. But more than that, it is the clan's. It is a way to heal.

I step in and walk in the water. I feel it rush past me and I become one with the waterfall. As I walk, the mist of soft colors engulfs me—pale pinks, pale yellows, pale lavender, a mist of blue and green.

As I step through the waterfall, I am in a familiar land. The trees, the grass, the birds, the walkway in front of me I recognize. Soft fog is all around. Out of the fog steps a warrior. He wears a loincloth of skin with hawk feathers hanging from it. On his bare chest is a bead plate chest guard made from the bone of the hawk. In the center of this chest plate are four hawk feathers and a hawk skull. All seven colors are present in the beads; they are handmade from clay and painted. The warrior's hands are huge and hold within them elk medicine. He extends his right hand, and in it he holds bones from an elk. He rolls his fingers around the bones and crushes them. He blows the soft powder on my hair. I feel the stamina of the elk as the bone powders my body and falls to the ground.

His left hand holds a long crystal rod. Inside it I see sparkling color, multitudes of yellow points of light. The rod turns a deep, rich purple with yellow lights inside it, running up and down. A vibrating force of light collects at the tip. He brings the rod up in front of him like a spear. As he holds it close to his face, I see his intense brown eyes. His face is shaped like a horse. His headdress is filled with hawk feathers, and four wolf teeth hang from each ear. He draws the rod back over his shoulder as if he is going to throw it. The deep, rich purple color within the crystal grows stronger as he aims it at me. He releases the rod and the power comes towards me!

I reach out with my left hand and catch the rod. It goes through the palm of my hand, up my arm and into my shoulder. The power bursts and surges through my body. I extend my right hand and out of my fingers come blue stars. I take a deep breath as the energy surges through my body to my feet, back up to my knees, up my spine and into my brain. Out of my right hand come more blue stars. As they hit the ground they break into tiny points of yellow light and flow across the ground as an oily substance, the color of gold. It moves over the rocks and down the hillside, creating a goldish-yellow path. The warrior turns his head slightly, and looks at me sharply out of one eye.

He speaks. "No path is easy. The path of creativity is one that you create. Ideal circumstances are yours. Draw from your vision the ability to walk that ideal. To create ceremony, to endure the circle of no beginning and no end, this is the point of yellow light known as the yellow star. Walk this path, one of discipline, the way to creativity. The answers shall follow as each step you paint, each word you write, each doorway you open. Create a magnitude, a multitude, a velocity. The ability to create the divine is yours."

The warrior disappears, leaving seven hawk feathers. I walk on the golden path towards them. As I bend to touch them, they turn into one yellow star that spins on its point. Smaller and smaller it becomes, until it lies flat on the ground. I pick it up, place the star in my medicine pouch and take a deep breath. I feel the power of the blue stars in my right hand. I am at one with the yellow star, creation, creativity, the sun, the Son. I stand on the golden road of yellow ochre and I know now. NOW. Now is the art. Now is the way. Now is the path. Now is always. The answers call me.

"You are right. It is good."

I feel this pulsating in my mind and I hear an answer, "A need to."

Rainbow Medicine

Everything around me becomes very light and airy, pale yellow. I see a mixture of greens. It is the tree people. One of them speaks with a very clear voice.

"When you have a vision, do you know what it means? Do you know what a 'need to' is?"

I am intrigued. I walk closer to the tree.

"Tell me more, tree person."

There is no answer. I hold the yellow star in my hand. An emptiness is there, and at the same time a fullness. I hear drumming in the woods and bells clanging. I walk through the small thicket of trees. I can smell smoke. Ahead of me I see a camp. The yellow-greenish skies around me are showing the first signs of a storm. I hear thunder in the distance.

Before me native people are gathering their children, loosening their horses, tightening their lodges. There is a circle of dancers. The beating of the drums and the dancing is very familiar, the same as the magnified beating of my heart. The thunder grows louder. With the yellow star in my hand, I walk closer to the people. Rain begins to fall and they disappear. All is gone. No people, no lodges. No song, no dancing. Just the rain and the thunder and the lightning. The sky grows darker and the rain falls thick and fast. I stand and let it wash me. So heavily the rain falls, I cannot see. My tears mix with the rain. I feel my sadness being washed away. And the rolling thunder echoes across the plains.

I stand alone on flat land as the rain falls harder and the thunder gets louder. I look at my right hand. Blue stars are dripping from my fingers, but on the ground, there is nothing. In my left hand I still hold my yellow star.

"Grandfather and Grandmother Spirit, Great Spirit, Creator, hear me. I call you, Grandfather. You have given me the sun, and the moon, and the seven stars. You have led me within the sun and shown me four directions. You have given me four doors to go through and lessons I've heard. You have gifted me with this marvelous spiritual place, a journey that takes me. Speak to me with your wisdom, and teach me what to do with my stars."

There is a reply, like thunder across the sky.

"Granddaughter Wolf, your vision is memory. You have the ability to walk within the sun and remember the story that brings forth a sacred walk. Granddaughter Wolf, it's yours to be the path bearer. It is of your blood and of your heart to show the way. Through your vision, you draw knowledge, and reflect it back in your daily walk. Within creativity, you listen to the two stars before you. Creativity consists of balance and confidence. Learning to read the color and listening to the stars is a walk of discipline."

Lightning breaks in forks all around me, and dances on the ground. Thunder cracks behind it. The rain is now light and easy. As the lightning strikes, it lights up the sky and I can see my surroundings.

"Granddaughter, do you have fear in your heart?"

"No, Grandfather, I have confidence. I have come to Grandfather Red Star, and I have found confidence. I have listened to Grandfather Orange Star, and I have found balance. I understand the difference between confusion and clarity. I stand with the yellow star in my hand, Grandfather, Great Spirit, not knowing what is next but feeling my creativity—a desire to make art and music, to tell the story, to write, to do and to be. Life is such a simple flow, Grandfather Spirit, and you have given us the chance to test each walk, each color, each word. I know this in my heart. I hear it from the tree people. They ask me if I know of my need. My need is to know more, Grandfather, of my vision. For you to teach me through the sight that you have given me, that I might take it to others that they might see more clearly. Grandfather Spirit, I believe this is my walk."

"Oh, Granddaughter Wolf, it is more than your walk. It is your calling. The wolf that you see within, do you know the story? Do you know the tale of the Wolf?"

I smile. "When you say the 'tale' of the Wolf, I only think of the 'tail' that hangs."

"We can start there, Granddaughter. The tail hangs on the wolf for balance. It gives the ability to balance. Is it beginning to sound familiar now? The head of the wolf, the very nose itself, gives it the confidence to sniff out and follow the path. To know the way is the alpha, to be able to seek out and find the answer when there is nothing but darkness. To make a good out of a bad. To take the two and make one, negative and positive. To bring about a flow, which is one.

"Granddaughter, you have an inherited ability to walk the range. So many two-leggeds wonder what the answers are. It has been given to you— on the outside a two-legged, on the inside a four-legged. On the inside of that, the color of burgundy. On the inside of that, clarity.

"This is you, little Granddaughter. This is the tale of the Wolf. You live this time as a two-legged, before that as a wolf, before that as a color, before that as a way."

At that moment, a large bolt of lightning strikes and the sky is lit with bright reds, oranges and yellows. Magenta, and pink, chartreuse, tangerine. The colors beside, behind and around the lightning pull me to my memory.

"Grandfather, is that your face I see?"

"Yes, Granddaughter Wolf. Look in my eyes. Look into the dark, the deeper shade of purple, and see my eyes."

Darkness begins to fall again after the lightning, and stillness. I see a large rock ahead of me. I crawl up and sit on it. Looking out over the prairie I see a river moving swiftly past. It shimmers in the sunset. The river speaks:

"Life flows downhill. It has its own pattern. You are a work of art that Great Spirit has created. I am a work of art that Great Spirit has created. Within the flow, the river, are many lessons. I have called you to my side, that you might listen and hear what I offer as a teacher. I have for you an encounter, one of grand yellow spirit. Come closer to me and I will show you."

I stand and walk closer to the water. It changes and I see a mountain scene. Snow on the mountains, a valley in front, a place where I stand and look out over large pines. An eagle soars overhead. It seems so familiar. I sit back on the rock and try to make sense of the river and the mountains.

"What is this I see? Speak again, River, so I may know."

There is only silence. The dark has come again, the deeper shade of purple with lightning in the distance. I sit quietly in the stillness, holding the yellow star in my hand. I open my hand and look at the yellow star.

"What sense do I make of all these things? How do I get the answers? Where do I find the knowledge?"

I Hear the Rapid Beat of the Drum Calling Me Back.

The Path Map

Needed: *A piece of white 100% cotton cloth or paper or deerskin 12 inches (30cm) square; paints*

On the skin, cloth or paper you will build a drawing that is your personal map to your goals. You will use this to work from in realizing them.

When you have seen your vision, you will have a group of symbols you can draw or objects you can attach that will represent your goals and help you achieve them. *Do not put words on your Path Map. A Path Map is a* visual way to follow your life dreams.

Paint each symbol on the map. Also make a written key and place all your medicine symbols in the key. This way, working from the key, you can make short-term goals and lists to achieve your vision. Your map is a lifetime project. If you choose, you can do 20-year maps. When the map is completed, you can attach it to a hoop and hang it in your room.

The hoop is a circle, made from any wood of your choice. It represents the four seasons, the totality of life. To attach your map, punch holes at the outer edge and then run string through them. Lace your map onto the hoop.

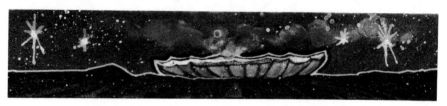

Understanding Your Creativity

Through my vision of Rainbow Medicine I bring to you suggestions learned through following my vision path. I feel it is very important to have a vision by which to understand your rites of spirituality. To be able to bring forth the fullness of a vision is the platform and foundation of human existence.

Understanding your creativity can be done in four steps or seven steps.

The Four-Step Process to Understanding Creativity

1. **The beginning.** Having an idea is a beginning and it brings anticipation. In thinking and anticipating, collect words that give form to

your ideas and goals. Structure these words into an outline. This outline also holds feelings.

2. **Feelings.** Throughout the creative process, journal your feelings and incorporate them into your outline. A journal is a very special tool that provides the space to reflect on personal feelings, to give structure to them, and to organize them in a good way. All this is necessary to achieve your goals. Your feelings need to be acknowledged in order for you to formulate the physical outline from which your path is constructed.

   Understand that feelings originate from the six basic human emotions: fear, anger, disgust, sadness, acceptance, and joy. Work with your feelings very carefully, asking where are my fears? What makes me angry? What disgusts me, and what do I need to be disgusted about? What makes me sad? What do I accept, what do I need to accept, and what don't I accept? What brings about grand joy?

3. **Goals.** Form a picture in your mind, a structure that you can see. Use your innate creativity to visualize and formulate your goals. Think them out carefully so that they can become tangible. Start by seeing what it is that you want to create. Bring it into form in your mind. Get a strong, clean picture.

   Example: See a piece of bare soil that you wish to turn into a flower garden. Visualize the ground turned over, rich and fertile, flowers growing and bark placed on top of the dirt with rocks to edge the perimeter.

Now examine your visualization very carefully and break it down into steps.

Example:
1. Select a good area where the plants will get proper sunlight and drainage.
2. Turn the soil.
3. Plant the seeds.
4. Water.
5. Weed, thin and keep working the garden as it grows and matures.
6. Add the ground cover and trim the edges with rocks. You have set up a ceremonial site.

It is important to set goals that are simple, and to structure them in a simple way. Then you are able to achieve them. Keep it simple.

4. **Outcome.** Visualization creates movement, first in the anticipation, then in the orchestration of feelings and events during goal-setting. This provides your power, allowing you to create in tangible form now. From this comes movement, the opportunity to go into a new cycle of events, to structure from raw focused energy a new creation.

Example: The flower garden is completed and you choose to plant herbs the following year. You decide to design your herb garden in a way that provides both cooking and scent herbs. The creative movement of adding the herbs provides new goals: it allows you to produce herb oils for salads, and oils for perfumes and potpourri.

Everything that you create is a movement. Therefore, you have the opportunity to keep moving in a full circle, spiralling into the next event from the event that has taken place.

The Seven-Step Process to Understanding Creativity

1. **Balancing.** Confidence is a primary factor in supplying the support needed to create. Make sure your confidence is based in purity.

Example: When I create, be it writing, design, painting, sewing, cooking, raising children—whatever the creative form—I have a total belief that the energy comes from Creator.

Equally important is to center yourself. This is done by accepting your own capabilities, your strengths and limits. The mind requires a great deal of energy to interpret and understand raw creativity. Your mind is only able to do this when the body's chemicals, including sugars, are in balance.

If you are not getting enough exercise, if your diet is wrong for you, if you suffer from sleep deprivation, eat too much sugar—causing highs and lows—are taking hallucinogenic drugs or are drinking too much alcohol, it is very hard for the brain to produce the energy necessary to orchestrate creative ideas.

To tap into your creativity and follow it through, it is imperative to have a personal daily routine of mental and physical organization. Formulate a rest, diet and exercise plan that works for you. Eliminate nicotine, drug and/or alcohol addictions. In the absence of addiction, limit the level of alcohol to two drinks per day.

2. **Safety.** Understand that your creativity is related to your location, and that safety is the balancing force necessary to bring about your

success. When you are safe, you have the ability to be correct and not to worry. A lack of worry is essential for creativity.

Select a place where you feel solid and safe, where you feel that the environment is giving back to you as you are giving to it. When you are being creative there should be a flow of choices and this should not be disrupted by anger or disputes. Structure your creative environment so that you do not feel vulnerable and are able to diffuse worry.

Support is necessary to build the confidence needed for balance, which is the platform of creativity. Our environment may support us in many ways—with views that inspire, people around us who are supportive of our efforts, and land that feels protected and loved. When we think of earth as a mother, we relate to her as a provider of safety, giving us non-threatening space.

3. **Communication with the spirit world.** Know the basis of what Creator energy, Great Spirit, Grandfather and Grandmother are to you. Having a connection to the spirit world and understanding the teachings, whether contemporary or traditional, is necessary for the beauty and power of your adventure within creativity. An active prayer life connects you to the power of faith that brings about creative constructions.

When you set your beliefs, they should be individual and based upon what you choose, formulated as your truth. The opportunity to choose and structure your belief system yourself allows you to achieve your creativity. Draw upon the power of your belief system and your understanding of Creator, whatever this may be. Understand that this is a necessary part of creativity.

As you learn from your teachers, remember that each word spoken by a teacher is as a leaf on a tree. The tree has a multitude of leaves and each one represents an opinion. An important part of creativity is to understand that leaves fall off and grow back in a constant cycle of loss and renewal. The stability of the tree is in the trunk and the roots. Thus the history of the leaves comes from what the tree is rooted in. Each leaf that falls to the ground supplies the space, the nutrients, and the recorded history that enables the tree to endure and cycle again.

4. **Structure.** Creativity has no beginning and no end. It is a full cycle of energy that you, as an individual, tap into and structure, bringing about a result in the physical realm. When outlining a project, understand that you are tapping into circle energy, that everything that goes around comes around.

Structure has four components:

1. To respect.
2. To hold sacred.
3. To be organized.
4. To display.

Remember that this is a constantly moving cycle. When you tap into it, understand the value of the adventures held within. Could it be that this cycle began with the two-leggeds, and that it is necessary to respect and be sacred in order to be fully creative?

Could it be that the two-legged's talent for organization, when expressed in a balanced way that is connected to Creator, is a good thing—good for our earth mother and for all our relations?

Could it be that the display of our finished products of creativity, whether accomplished individually or collectively, enriches the flow of creativity? That honoring these accomplishments actually adds to the energy flow? We have the grand opportunity to understand this in our daily practice of life.

5. **Joy.** The supply of energy necessary to be truly creative for the long haul stems from joy. One needs to be able to enjoy (be "in-joy") before one can truly understand creativity.

   Your joy has your truth at its root. Enjoy what you are doing while you are doing it. This is at the core of the accomplishments of creativity. When I received my vision as a child, it was an adventure. I look at my whole life as an adventure. There have been many rough times in my earth walk as a person, but the ability to experience joy has been at the base root of my successes.

6. **Knowledge.** Motivation is the first movement of knowledge. The ability to care comes from being motivated. When feelings are acknowledged, respected, honored and worked with, their energy is clearly transformed into motivation. There is a strong connection between motivation and the creative force.

   For many activities, pure survival is the motivation. Creativity, however, requires a spiritual or philosophical belief, whatever it may be, that provides a foundation for the experience. Without this foundation, the experience of creativity is null and void, for there must be an avenue by which one reaches within the spiritual realm to tap the energy needed to achieve the finished creative product.

   The second movement of knowledge is the wisdom that comes from pure experience, which begins as desire. A watercolor painter, for example, has the desire to enjoy watercolors as an art form. Desire takes you within the experience of the medium itself, stimulating your perception. This in turn feeds your ability to visualize creatively.

Visualize the finished product and enjoy it. Do this before you begin, so that you can see the result. In this way, creativity is a spiralling flow, a cycle, with no beginning and no end.

Responsibility is the closing movement of knowledge. The best way to understand creative responsibility is to think of a mother and father giving birth to a baby. The baby will be a facet of their existence. Each thing that you create is a piece of what and who you are.

7. **Form.** The manifestation, the deliverance, the finished product. Realize that beyond this, the spiral continues. From each point, a new adventure takes place, because we are designed in a circular, spiralling way, continuously changing. The only thing consistent about Creator is change.

All things are the beginning of an adventure in creativity.

Aho.

· 11 ·
The Green Star

Before me I see a path. I breathe in and out. I step on this path, knowing that I'm in search of the green star. I have a grand anticipation and wonder what the green star will teach me. The path before me is straight. The ground is solid and hard. I take another deep breath and start to walk.

The objects that grow here are unlike any I've seen. They look like wavy lines, curved and angular objects, like metal growing from the ground. Before me I see something flying. It has wings in place of legs. It has eyes where its wings are supposed to be. It has scales and hair made from a metallic substance. As the light hits it, it shimmers. It has a horn from its rear and a tail from its mouth. An unusual creature.

I continue on the path, studying the objects that I pass. They seem to be alive, but they look like metal. The land around me is silver, grey, blah. This is a strange place. On the left of the path I see something that is similar in size to a horse. As I approach I see that it has a plastic skin. Instead of ears, it has objects that look like doorknobs. Its feet look like bathroom plungers. Pointed objects that look like carrots are where its eyes would go. It turns its head. It's alive. Its hair is grass. Okay!

I walk on. Ahead, something is moving towards me. The front of it has straight black lines running parallel.

It is similar to an automobile but it looks as if it's made out of stone, a brown shiny substance. Four metal-like poles stick out from the top. In it there is a being with red lights for eyes and pieces of wire for a mouth. This is a very unusual place. The object moves past me, smoke coming from behind it.

I continue walking. Beside me is a substance that we would call dirt. I bend to touch it. It quivers like Jell-O. I pull my hand up, and it sticks to my fingers, a yellow, orangish, green-tinted, stretchy gum. Then it releases from my hand and snaps back down to what we would know as the ground.

All around me now is a soft green mist. It smells like sulfur burning the inside of my nostrils. Maybe I'm in a toxic waste area. Maybe my vision comes from a bad pickle I had on a hamburger. Hmmm.

Oh, no! I shouldn't have thought that—in front of me I see this object appearing from the mist. It's a large hamburger. It has wings. Its mouth and face look like a turtle. No. I don't use drugs!

I take a deep breath. I let it out. Nope, the hamburger hasn't gone away. Its face looks like a friendly turtle with freckles. Its feet are similar to an elephant's and it has an odd walk. Its front two feet go to the left, while its back two feet go to the right.

I continue past the hamburger, noticing it has a tail like a pig. What an unusual place.

I see an opening ahead in the mist. It appears to be a cave. I step through it into darkness. I feel myself walking down as I go further into the cave. The color around me is a deep, dark shade of purple and blue. I can barely see my hand in front of my face. I continue to walk downward. I see a light ahead of me, a pale, shimmering green light. Water is beginning to trickle down the side of the tunnel. It's cavern water, and it forms a stream beside me as I walk towards the shimmering green light. The stream gets wider and I follow it. The water is an iridescent green. I hear small puff sounds as I get to the end of the cavern, into an opening where soft green light is now a reality.

In front of me is a vastness of mountains, with puffy clouds. There are green pines everywhere. The terrain seems to be normal. I hear a giggling sound.

"Normal?" this voice says. "You haven't looked very well."

Mmmm. I continue to look and it seems to be normal terrain—grass, rocks, trees. "It seems normal to me."

"Normal?" The voice gurgles as it speaks. "Look again."

"Where are you? I don't see who speaks to me."

"Oh well, you're looking for normal. You wouldn't be able to see me," it laughs. "I'm not normal."

"Well, I'll stop looking for you, because you're bothering me. I see normal. The sky is blue. The clouds are white and puffy. I see a tree—it's growing from the ground; it has its base connected to the ground and around it is grass and rock and dirt, and that constitutes normal. The trees look like pines to me and they seem to be on the side of the hill that's at the base of the mountain. It looks very normal."

"If it's so normal, why can't you see me?"

"Well, because you're a figment of my imagination and I'm only imagining you. I'm only imagining all of this."

"No, I don't think that's so. I don't think you've looked carefully. Watch, I'll show you . . ."

And everything went dark. There was nothing. No sky. No clouds. No trees. Just black.

"Now, is that normal? Does that look normal to you? Wasn't it daylight just a minute ago?"

Before me I see pairs of little green eyes staring in the dark. Two sets of green here, two sets of green there. There are green eyes over my back, over my shoulder, above my head and all around me—hundreds of little points of green light. Then, once again, it is the mountains, the sky and the trees.

"There. Looks quite normal, doesn't it?"

"Right," I reply. "I am on the path. Maybe If I tell you what I'm looking for, you'll help me."

"I don't know if help is what I am."

"You can try, though, and see. I'm looking for a green star. You probably have one on your body somewhere because each teacher I've encountered so far has."

"Teacher? What's that?"

"Ummm, each spokesman that carries the star that allows me to know what I need to know."

"Nope, that's not me. I don't know anything. Don't have any stars. Don't have any of those things. It's not normal to have stars. If I had a star, I wouldn't be normal, so you know it's not me because you are looking for normal."

"Right," I reply. "I'm continuing on my path, I think. I'm going on up ahead and leaving you now, if you don't mind."

"Ha, ha, ha," is the reply. "I don't think so. I don't think leaving me is normal."

Rainbow Medicine

"I don't think you know what normal is," I say.

"Oh, yeah. I know it's quite normal not to leave me. There isn't any way you can leave me."

I have had enough of this conversation with whatever. . . . I see sage along the path as I walk, something I recognize as a normal, growing plant. The smell is strong and rich. I enjoy the sage. It reminds me of ceremony. I come upon a valley with a rambling, small river. Two hawks fly overhead, joined by a raven. They circle above me. It feels familiar—large, white puffy clouds in the sky and the mountain terrain. The hills beside me are shades of green—soft greens, grey greens, mixed in with the solid greens of the pines. Everything is back into balance and very normal.

"Nooooo. Not normal." The voice again.

"I demand that you reveal yourself."

"Nope. Don't want to reveal myself. That's not normal."

"Why is it that you're following me and taunting me about normal?"

"Taunting? Who's taunting? I'm not normal. If anybody's taunting anybody, you're taunting me. You're pushing. You're always pushing. You don't stop pushing."

"Either reveal yourself and tell me who you are, or go."

"I don't go, either. I'm always. I gather enjoyment from watching you seek normal. If normal is so important to you, then why are you in the land of the abnormal?"

"The land of the abnormal?" I ask.

"Right. Didn't you notice as you came in that things are not like you're used to? Didn't you notice the scrushees and the lababoos? You went right through the pedabows and didn't pay any attention to 'em."

"Okay, so you have your own language and I'm in a place that's not normal."

"Oh, not normal compared to what? Why do you seek normality? Is it because you're uncomfortable? Does it frighten you to be in a place that you cannot control?"

"Well, you know, it isn't every day you see a talking, flying, walking hamburger."

"Oh, well. It's not every day that you're in the land of growth, either. It's not every day that you're in a place where you can't control things. Because you don't accept growth. You don't accept the power of faith. It's a mystery to you and that's why you're here. You've come to the underworld. You've come to the place where the Lower exists.

"It's funny, on earth, how everything that is lower is referred to as evil—scary, backward, abnormal, mentally deranged, confused. When really, all we are is growth. The experience of abnormality, walked through on a daily basis, becomes accepted as familiar. Don't you like growth?"

"Well, I never thought about being in the land of growth. I'm looking for the green star."

"Right. You're looking for the green star. Did you think it would be a green path with a bunch of four-leaf clovers? You know, this vision that you have is not just yours. It isn't something you can have and then put in your pocket and keep forever. It's a reality. And reality has two sides: the side of acceptance, which comes easily, and the side of turmoil, which comes hard."

As I listen to the voice, I see a very large mountain, soft pale blue. Above it is a spirit keeper, a cloud that forms a buffalo head: a white buffalo keeps the spirit of the mountain. The buffalo looks over the mountain as if it is its own child. Further away I see a herd of buffalo standing in reverence of the one that watches over the mountain. It is a wonderful thing, to gaze into the clouds and see the spirit keeper of the mountain.

"You do realize that it took growth to achieve the ability to see that," the voice goes on. "Most people would just look at it as a cloud. On earth, people call it study. It is from the underworld that the imagination produces the creative flow that allows fantasy to exist within the two-legged. From the underworld comes everything that is unusual. Here, it is possible to walk on the sky and to see through the ground.

"Let me take you some place where you can see me more clearly."

"Nope. I'm not going anywhere with you, 'cause I can't see you at all. Where I'm used to being, I see normal and understand normal," I reply.

"Well, it's going to take more than normal for you to be able to understand. And understanding is what you seek, to step through to the wisdom of the blue star. But you have yet to find your green star and to understand what growth truly is. So you have to go into the underworld, deeper within the realm of imagination, to create the flight of the hawk. To understand the walk of the deer. To listen to the movement of the cat. To know the thought of the bear. To think as the fox, and to be as the wolf. This is what you seek in asking for the green star. Do you choose to follow or not?"

Steady on my path now, the surroundings begin to change. Blissful color, swirling patterns are inviting me with soft movements to come towards . . . Then I see the form of a beautiful woman with wings. She is radiantly gorgeous. She expands her wings and draws them in and out. She dances around me, her wings light and airy. All colors dance in her wings. I sit on a rock nearby and watch the dance. Each stroke of her wings sends out sparks of color—oranges and greens, purples and blues, blacks and whites. Pale yellows. Reds. Her face is timeless, pale, transparent with small, defined features.

She glides above my head in circles, soaring into the clouds, circling, spinning, dancing in the sky. I watch in amazement as more of her kind begin to fly. They soar in the air. Hundreds of them. All points of light, all colors, all softness, all around me.

"Now is this normal?" I hear the voice.

"I don't know. I think I'm beginning to get used to unusual."

As I watch the flying creatures around me, a soft breeze carries in the scent of lilac and lavender. The pungent smell of the lavender invokes my attitude of acceptance.

"I think I'm accepting of unusual."

There is a sigh from the voice. "This is a good thing. To accept the unusual is the first passage to growth. There are four passages you must make to achieve the green star."

One of the flying creatures becomes very small, a normal-sized butterfly. Yet I can see the face of what you know as a two-legged. It lands on my shoulder, walks down my arm and does somersaults on my hand. Standing on my fingers, she speaks.

"I will be your guide, taking you through the realms. I will show you the rites, the passages of growth. I will give you a name you will know me by in your mind. I will touch your mind with the ability to know the spirit names of all. I will give you the gift of name-giving, if you can give me my name."

"It's very simple. Your name is Butterfly Woman. It's easy to know that. I see you as you are, Butterfly Woman."

"This name, Butterfly Woman, that you call me. Why do you call me that? Butter fly? What is this butter fly? What is woman?"

The look in her eye challenges me. For a moment I want to feel wrong. I sense myself a failure. But I remember the red star. No, I won't budge, Butterfly Woman. I take a breath, center myself and focus. I remember the lessons of the orange star.

"It is Butterfly Woman. I know that to be your name. What is butterfly woman? It is the smoothness that butter represents. Smooth, soft. Fly is movement. Soft movement. Woman is legacy, bringing forth and carrying on. This is how I see you. Smooth, soft legacy. Movement. You are Butterfly Woman."

Her tiny eyes close and open and she smiles. "You're right. Soft ways are what I know myself as. Butterfly Woman is a good name. To you I give the gift of the name giver. You must always remember it is easy. It is simple. More than that, and it can cost you your red star."

She takes off in a burst of lights—delicate lights connected together in a band no wider than an inch. She darts about the sky, breaks into seven and then becomes one, turning and spinning on.

"Follow me." Her movement is quick in the air.

Ahead of me the path looks dark, almost foreboding, frightening. A feeling comes over me of not wanting to move on the path. I hesitate. Then I hear whispering sounds and smell mimosa trees in the springtime. Something wants to hold me and not let go—contain me, and not let me be. I break from that feeling and follow the faint light of Butterfly Woman.

I follow the trail quickly, admiring the colors of the stones on both sides that seem to be large chunks of crystal. I come to an opening where the light intensifies to yellow-green. I can hear rattling and the movement of bells, twinkling sounds mixed with a gourd rattle and a flute playing gently.

Inside the cavern ahead of me, I see Butterfly Woman, enlarged to human form, dancing around the fire. An old woman sits nearby. I stop in the doorway, hesitantly. The door does not seem mine to enter. I recall the word "passages." The rim around the door becomes movement. In front of my eyes are snakes, interwoven, forming the doorway. Entwined. Tangled. Moving.

I hear the soft words of the old woman. "Immersement. The passage of immersement. Dare you?"

She opens her hand and extends her long, narrow finger and beckons me on. "Dare you?"

I feel the need to spin. I raise my arms to the creature and spin in a clockwise movement. As I pass through the doorway I immerse myself in the energy of the snakes. I feel a transformation taking place, as if I am eternally different. Immediately within, I sit, quietly watching Butterfly Woman dance around the old woman.

"The rites of immersement. The passage of emerging."

From the fire come white butterflies. Small and fast, they fill the room, spiralling around as the snakes slide to the floor and make their way to the fire. Within the fire, they disappear. The white butterflies disperse and the room empties. Butterfly Woman sits on the old woman's shoulder. There is a timeless look in the old woman's eyes. She speaks.

"Enter. Growth has begun. Two passages you have found. Two shall you know."

I hear a rattle shake rapidly, as if a rattlesnake is at my feet. I look down. Only dirt. I look back and the old woman is gone. The room is empty. Only the trail of light is left that follows Butterfly Woman. I move once again on the path, following the soft shimmer of light. Up ahead a grove of willow trees sways in the breeze. The air is heavy and warm. I need a rest; I am sleepy and yet wide awake at the same time. I see the trail of light clearly in front of me, leading into the willow grove.

I walk into the grove, where there are hundreds of trees. The wind blows gently and the tree limbs sway above my head. On one of the limbs I see Butterfly Woman, sitting with her legs crossed and one of her wings dipped, a smile on her face.

"What is this you feel?"

And an echo from behind, a familiar voice, calls out, "Is it normal?" It laughs.

"Butterfly Woman, can you tell me whose voice that is?"

"Oh, you'll know soon. Once you have entered the fourth passage of growth, you will know."

The wind blows the limbs on the willow trees more fiercely. They sway to and fro and disappear. I stand in a barren desert, the sun pounding on my neck. In the distance I hear the song of the coyote, a yipping. I feel lonely and full at the same time. There are coyote tracks in front of me, etched in the light dust of the Butterfly Woman. I follow them. It seems a whole day has passed, following these tracks in the light dust. I come upon a small pond, where the tracks stop. The dust goes on over the pond and seems to disappear inside. I gaze into the small pond and there I see Butterfly Woman.

"The passage of choice. You have that. You have that right within growth, always, to make directional change. It's a split-second choice you need now."

From behind me comes a tremendous wind. It grows stronger each second. The sound is fierce. I look behind me and the sky has blackened in clouds. An awesome storm at my back, a pond in my face. A choice is necessary. As lightning strikes the ground just behind me, I leap into the pond. Immediately as I enter the pond, I exit on the other side. I feel myself rising, floating. Before me is a ridge of mountains. Gentle flute music echoes through the valley. Hawks circle slowly and easily in the sky. Clouds intertwine. A stillness of sun casts shadows on the ridges.

I no longer sense the depth of the underworld. I feel I have passed above into the realm of spirit. I see coyote tracks in the path in front of me. This time they show running movement. The coyote is moving faster towards the mountains. It is late afternoon.

A pass in the mountains calls me. As I enter it, the terrain is sloped and hilly. It invites me with its soft, sloping pattern and lumps and bumps of a yellowish-green, gentle color. The mystery of finding the next passage draws me on. I can feel the last passage—the choice. I have the ability to stop at any moment and bring myself home, but the excitement that lies ahead of me makes my heart pound.

As I enter the hills, I sense a feeling of older times. Wagon wheels are turning. I have the desire to remain forever. I come upon a grove of cottonwood trees where I rest in the sun, in the stillness. An elderly native man, maybe of Spanish descent, appears from behind a rock by the cottonwood grove. Around his shoulders he has a serape of many colors.

"We've been waiting for you. You have come to the fourth passage of growth. It is known as belief. You will know that you have your vision when you stand in the cottonwoods again. To go through the passage of belief, a choice is always made. To the wolf you must give your most precious thing, to achieve your belief. To know what that most precious thing is, you will sit this evening as the sun falls with Grandmother Green Star. She awaits you on the other side of the hill. Through the pass she lives. By your belief, your faith will carry you quickly. You will join her this evening. She will speak to you of growth, where faith is built from."

His spirit fragments in front of me and he disappears in the wind. Leaving the cottonwood grove, I walk along a dry river bed, once again noticing the tracks of the coyote in the light dust path. A sadness comes over me, I miss Butterfly Woman. Walking alone has an emptiness that opens a doorway in my feelings. I pay attention to the rock people, the grass people, the tree people. They speak to me as I walk.

"Do you understand the value of life-bearing? Do you know the qualities of being normal? Do you know the path of growth, how it starts? These are the questions that Grandmother Green Star is going to ask, and it will be yours to give her an answer, as you named Butterfly Woman. The transition, the transformation, is necessary for you to obtain the green star."

The path ahead of me begins to glisten and dance with color. Soft violets, pale lavenders, turquoise and green, pale blue and soft orange. Colors swirl tight to the path, low to the ground. Mystic hues of the light dust trail of Butterfly Woman. I feel myself coming close to what I would call home, where I would feel safe and understood—almost as if time didn't exist, and it had always been the way it was, and would always be the way it is.

Before me is a dirt drive that extends up into the hills. On the driveway I see a scraggly old coyote, hair pulled from its body, mangy. Its eyes are familiar, tired. Its tail hangs limp, its tongue longs for the taste of water. Slowly it ambles ahead of me up the drive, inviting me to follow. A dusty road it is, just a plain old road. The coyote lopes ahead of me, almost dancing. Beside the road a creek rolls along. I smell a mixture of dirt and sage.

The road climbs upward, moving through a rocky terrain. The old coyote disappears around the bend, back into the hills. By now my heart is pounding. I know I must be near the home of Grandmother Green Star. I can tell I am getting close. The greens are beginning to get richer, the air is thinner. Around me are white pines standing still.

Do I know what a life-bearer is? Do I know what normal is? I breathe in softly. I see before me a cave, just as the sun falls and the mountains turn many shades of dark purple. The tracks of the coyote etched in the light dust enter the cave. Past the doorway I see a shimmer of light. I step through into a misty green. There is a fire, and the flames dance off the walls of the cave. Stacks of wood, bent and twisted pieces of pinyon and scrub pine, lie in a pile. A green striped blanket is spread by the fire. I see a rattle, a drum, some feathers and a couple of bags. There is a tripod with a pot cooking over the fire. Coyote tracks are all around.

"Hellooooo," I call. "Hello, Butterfly Woman, are you here? Are you in this cave with me? Butterfly Woman, I see your tracks. I know you're in here."

"But you don't know if you're normal or not, do you?" a familiar voice says. "Have you decided what normal is? Is it pursuing your dream? Is it your vision? Have you made sense of the sun and the stars and the moon yet? Has it become familiar to you? Do you know what normal is?"

Out of the shadows steps an old woman. She is hunched and small, her face withered, her hair greyish-white and pulled back in a tight bun. I notice her hands; her fingers look like claws, shaped like a coyote's paw. She steps closer to the fire and I see the scruffy old tail that hangs behind her. Her eyes are rich, deep green. Her face is pale yellow, timeless. Her kindness is stiff, her mannerisms jerky. She seems a bit disconnected.

"Why don't you sit a while, and tell me what normal is," she says. "You seem to worry about that. Sit on the green blanket there, and we'll talk."

I sit cross-legged by the fire. The old woman draws her blanket around her, sits and pokes a stick in the flames. Out of the flames appears Butterfly Woman. She flies straight up, makes four circles and disappears through the cave top. I am sad that she is gone; a tear comes to my eye.

"That looks pretty normal to me," old woman says.

"What is your name?" I ask.

"I am Green Star. Grandmother Green Star."

"Each one of the spirits that I have met here as teachers are called stars. The first three were male, and now you're a female."

She nods. "And so will the other three be," she replies.

I look at her body carefully. I can't see the green star. It isn't on her nose, it isn't in her eyes. It isn't in her fingertips. A devilish grin comes over her face. She glances sideways and looks at me.

"Looking for the star, I suppose. You haven't earned it yet. It isn't that easy. Obtaining the green star is not tonight. It's not now. It's not within your grasp to rush within my den and find your green star. You must seek out the truth, and you must be wise. When you have shown me the seven responsibilities of impeccability, then I will gift you your green star. I will give you a clue. It is where the cottonwoods grow. It is the tale . . ."

And she stops, raises her left eyebrow, twitches her nose and smiles that strange smile. She stirs the pot that is hanging on the fire, pours something into a cup and hands it to me.

I ask, "What is this?"

"Something you'll like. Drink it." She nods her head up and down.

"No way! I'm not drinking this!"

She says, "Well, why not? Don't you want to know what something is? Heh, heh, heh," she laughs.

"No, I don't want to know what something is. I've been jerked around enough! This place is confusing enough!"

"Ah, you seek to know what normal is, but you don't have enough guts to find out what *something* is."

She stands up. I feel as if I have offended her. She moves away, back into the shadows, and disappears.

"You'll learn, when something's offered, to have faith. You'll learn not to turn your back and walk away. A greater teacher than I will come your way. One who will test you in everything that you have learned. Through your growth as a two-legged, you're required to find the answers."

"Wait," I call to her. "Before you go, can you tell me where the green star is? I must know what the green star is."

The voice grows fainter.

"I have told you. It's about faith, and to have faith you'll have to grow. There are four things to remember when you pursue your faith through growth. One is to be open. Two is to have insight. Three is not to give up. Four is to be able to relate.

"I give you this in honor of the green star, but growth will carry you through a road that will test your faith."

It grows dark around me. Absence. Alone. If I could reach out and change things, I'd make it more fun. I'd make it have more meaning. I travelled all this way, and no green star. I get up in the dark and leave the cave. Soft green mist surrounds me. It becomes lighter and the greenness softer. I walk out under a bright blue sky.

I Hear the Rapid Beat of the Drum Calling Me Back.

Rainbow Medicine

The Talking Stick Circle

The Talking Stick Circle is a place to go when you want to clear your mind and make good, sound decisions.

Needed: *As many talking sticks (see pages 63–64) as you need. All kinds of wood works. The sticks can be all shapes.*

Draw a circle 7 feet (2.1m) in diameter in the dirt, or place cornmeal, or draw a circle in the dirt. Put the stick or sticks on the ground around you as you sit in the circle. Come to the circle to listen to your mind, to listen to your emotions and feelings, to understand your needs. Focus on a stick and listen to your thoughts.

> *Example:* A long, straight stick—I feel the understanding I need will be long and hard. I have a long time to understand my mind and my thoughts. Time is long, answers are straight.

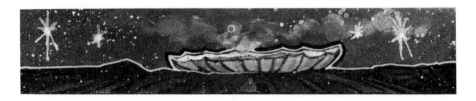

The Ceremony of Growth

For the ceremony of growth I suggest that you take no more than what you can carry in a backpack. I suggest that you say good-bye to everyone you know, as if you would never see them again. Take a sum of money; you can pick a number. Take your life-support things in the backpack—toothbrush, underwear, medicine objects—and leave your familiar surroundings. Let go of your family, your moms and your dads, your brothers and your sisters. Very similar to what Jesus said, pack up what you need, give away or sell everything else. Then walk away and follow your faith.

Keep your plan, your creative visualization that connects you to your vision, and leave, hit the road. Be it for a week, a month, a year. I suggest at least six months. To understand what true growth is takes being in the inner city, being on the road, and being out in the wilderness by yourself. To encounter your faith, you must face your fear. Facing your fear brings about growth.

Other suggestions in the ceremony of growth are to take on new adventures: learning how to drive a sports car when you usually drive a small car that saves money on gasoline; learning how to sail a boat when you don't even swim; learning how to ride a horse when you're afraid of falling.

Give up a large sum of money when you're used to being rich, and become poor. Give up being poor and take on monetary responsibility. Give up a job which has low status to take a high-paced, high-stepping position.

Facing growth is rolling with the flow, riding the river and understanding where it takes you. The key component of the ceremony of growth is always to know that you are within your vision. Keep your eyes open.

The steps beyond this point in the ceremony of growth are:

1. **Make seven prayer ties.** Touch base with Great Spirit by sitting down and making seven prayer ties (see pages 74–75). Tie them in a tree and leave them with your prayer that you grow and that you understand that growth.

2. **Make the quest for growth.** Take the adventure, the growth ceremony, go on the quest for growth. Expand your base beyond what is familiar to you.

3. **Journal.** During this growth quest, journal all your feelings. Keep every thought organized. What are the spots that feel most comfortable? What are the places that scare you the most?

4. **Connect to the spirit world by journey work.** Sit down where it's quiet, take four breaths and look for a familiar path in front of you in your mind. This will take you to the spirit world, where you will contact your animal, your personal shaman self and spirits that wish to talk to you and guide you. Making it personal is what is necessary to fulfill the spirit of the ceremony of growth.

After you have endured the ceremony of growth, take seven full days to analyze what has happened. Read your journal and see what you have connected to. Look at the vastness, look at the expansion of creativity that you have at your fingertips. You are capable of things that you never would have thought possible: going into the depth of a large city, or outside civilization, walking with strangers, and eating and sleeping in a new place. Going with the flow. Understanding the connection of the whole circle, the process. Seeing those who don't know what they're doing, and those who do. Being able to stay focused in your own center and knowing your own self. All this is part of your growth.

Most important, give respect back to Great Spirit, Grandfather, Grandmother, for taking care of you and protecting you, for guiding you to the right paths and bringing you back to your truth.

Aho.

· 12 ·
The Blue Star

I breathe in and out. Before me I see a familiar, rugged path over rough terrain. The path has ridged crevices, as though a four-wheel drive had plowed through the mud, which is now hard. It's in a mountain setting. I see different shades of blue from steel grey to midnight, as the sky begins to darken around me.

Walking along the path ahead of me is an old man, slowly shuffling his feet up the road. He's wearing baggy khaki pants, a loose-fitting burgundy flannel shirt and a straw hat with little balls dangling from the edges. He walks with a cane. I quickly catch up with him.

"Sir. Sir, excuse me. Can you tell me what path I'm on, or where I'm headed?"

He looks at me and his face is of rock, the lines and crevices deep. His eyes are steel blue.

"Well, sure, I can tell you what road you're on, missy," he says slowly.

"You're on the path to truth. You're heading towards the blue stars, the place of healing. You're going to pass one of the most powerful places, the Pond of Reflection. The still waters of reality are on this path. Many come around here seeking the river that leads to the Pond of Reality: a place where people come to find their proof, to seek out their clarity. This is the path that you're on."

I look at the old man's feet, the colors of multi-shaded rock. He wears sandals on his rock feet. Soft white hair sticks out from under his odd old hat. A unique man.

"Yep. You're on the path, here, the path to truth."

As we walk, four ravens circle above our heads and then spin out in all four directions.

"Well, I'm glad to know that I'm on the right path, because I have to find the blue star and understand its teachings, and also a purple star and a burgundy star before I can truly have and understand my green star. I was told by Grandmother Green Star that it's necessary to have all this in order to have growth."

"Well, I've run into her more than once," the old rock-faced man says, "and she's true about that. Why don't we walk along a ways and you can share with me, maybe, some of your stories about your truth."

The path is steep; the climbing is rough and you'd think it would be hard to travel this terrain. But it is very easy. It seems as if we just move up the hill. As we climb, the trees thicken. There are many pines. The bright blue sky above is becoming a deep, rich, evening blue.

"Well, I don't have a lot to speak of, other than that I've had great experiences following my confidence. I'd have to say that my truth, more than anything, is my vision. Understanding my vision is why I've come here to the spirit land. It's what I seek more than anything."

"Well, don't you have any truths," he asks, "like wanting to have children while you're a two-legged, or wanting to have a lot of money and live in a fancy home? Don't you have a truth you believe in more than anything?"

"No, I'm not sure that I do. You know, what's going on back in my world is war and people rebelling against each other, saying they're going to save the earth and maybe we can slow down crime. I don't see those things as truths. I don't see them happening. It seems rather like it's always going to be individuals seeking out what's necessary for themselves. I guess if I had to say I had a truth, that would be it. By the way, do you have a name?"

I glance over at the old rock-face man, but he is gone.

I look at the path up ahead of me, and its roughness. The climb seems to be getting harder and night is coming. I remember Grandmother Growth,

Grandmother Green Star. Maybe if I were to climb in the night, it would be a growth ceremony. Maybe it would bring up characteristics in me that I don't know.

I keep going, stepping on the rocks, slipping and sliding, working hard, climbing. In front of me, sitting on a rock, is a young man. He has on blue jeans, hiking boots with red shoestrings and a flannel shirt, unbuttoned. Beneath it I see a blue tank top. His long flowing, wavy brown hair is pulled back by a red bandana. He wears dark glasses. He is mysterious-looking. A brown beard. He is holding a walking stick. The closer I come, the more familiar he seems.

"Good evening," he says.

It is odd to see someone sitting beside a path out in the middle of nowhere, wearing dark glasses in the night. I stop.

"Where are you headed?" he asks.

"I'm following the path, looking for a blue star, maybe many blue stars."

"Blue stars? You know, I've seen those in the sky. I've seen them fall from the sky, too. Hit the ground. There's a pond up ahead, not far, known as the Blue Star Pond. It's said by the native peoples and by spirits, that falling stars made the pond. From this pond we leave and go on our earth walk. Then, from this pond we come here to spirit land where we share the stories of our journey."

I notice that beside his feet lies an old yellow dog, relaxed, not even moving. Just resting.

"I'm going that way," he says. "If you want me to guide you, I'll show you the way to the pond where the blue stars fell from the sky."

We walk together. There is something magical about this person—a spirit within his spirit. For a few minutes it seems as if he is real, that he is a real two-legged. The night grows darker and the sounds of the owl are around us in the forest. Beside us is a wide river now, with boulder rock in it, with pine and rough terrain all along its banks. We stay on the path, walking in the night. Up above is a full moon.

"That there's my grandmother," he says as he looks up at the moon. "She teaches me a lot of things and she guides me in the night. It's never dark when Grandmother's there. Sometimes when we walk in the night, we feel as if it's dark and we're all alone. There's something about being a human that make us think that when it's night, when it's dark, therefore we're alone. And we get scared when we're two-legged. But that's not how it is here in the spirit world. Grandmother shines her light of blues and the truth echoes around us. Why, you can even see fish moving in the river."

I look closely and see trout run past. The moonlight bounces off the rocks and shoots back in my guide's eyes. There I see two blue stars twinkling. For a moment I think that I have met Grandmother Blue Star, but I remember Grandmother Green Star telling me that the last four colors would be women. But I know I saw the blue stars in his eyes. The light bounces through his dark glasses and I see into his soul. There I see a feeling—what we two-leggeds call love. The reflection of the moon and the water in his eyes invite me within to a space that I have never known, deep and fast. I draw closer, reach out and put my hands on his shoulders. He isn't there. With my eyes I can see him—but I can't touch him.

He turns and steps out on a rock in the river. He dances onto four or five of them, moving across the stream from me.

"I'm not to be held or touched," he says. "It's like putting a bear in a cage. There is no way to house a bear in a cage and not kill it. Bears are meant to run through the woods. They're not to be caged and owned. This walk you take with me tonight, as we step on the stones, is known as a moon dance. The moon dances across the water and the water runs the rocks. And it flows. You'll take your moon dance and earn your name. You'll understand that your ancestry is the moon dance. To hold on to me would simply stifle your life.

"Up the river is a cabin where you'll find the doorway to your spirit. You'll encounter Grandmother, and before the sun rises you'll know the truth that lives in the spirit of love. Follow me."

And he darts across the rocks to the swifter water. It is deep and fast. The rocks are slippery, and it is scary.

"I can't do this, I can't—I can't walk on the rocks in the river in the night. I'm not you. I don't have your knowledge."

A stillness comes from within me. Grandfather Spirit's voice says, "It isn't knowledge you see. It's the truth. What is it he does that you can't?"

I watch him dance across the rocks, his feet doing a criss-cross pattern. He works his way up the river ahead of me.

"He does, Grandfather, he just does."

"That's right, and so can you. Now follow him up the river, Granddaughter Wolf. Don't hesitate. That's the key to truth—not hesitating. Those moments of hesitation stifle the flow of growth. Right there is doubt, and then you only have doubt."

I watch this man dance the rocks, moving upstream with the water. I start to follow, one rock at a time. I feel my feet begin to criss-cross and move like my guide's—quickly across the rocks, into the deeper rapids, moving from boulder to boulder. I look at the silver moonlight shimmering on the water. I hear the rush of the river beside me. Not once does fear stop me. I dance for miles on the river that night. I feel ageless, as though I will always be 19. Time is nothing here.

My guide jumps from the rocks, hits the bank and disappears into the woods. He leaves his shirt by the bank. I hit the bank and grab his shirt. I hold it in my hands and within my spirit. He is real. I follow him into the woods, and there I see the footprints of a man. I follow as they transcend, becoming a bear's. I follow the footprints for miles in the woods, seeking the one who wore this shirt. I come to a den, a very dark cave, in the early morning. Within I hear a growl, the awesome roar of a black bear. I am face to face with shiny white teeth. I look in his eyes and remember what he has said, "You can not own me or put me in a cage."

I put on the shirt and walk on a path that leads away from the cave. A cute little hand-carved sign says "3 miles to Grandmother's." I smell coffee, an inviting fragrance. The sun begins to crack through the dawn. I smell fresh trout cooking. I can even hear the crackling sounds of grease in a skillet. There is a chill in the morning. I blow smoke with my breath.

I see a little log cabin, with a porch of big brown log pillars. An old yellow dog lies by the porch. I step up and read a carving, "David and [somebody]." It isn't finished. I can't make out the girl's name, just David plus. It is carved into a pillar of the porch. I take another step. Gazing at the blue door gives me a feeling like family. It is Grandmother Blue Star's.

Suddenly, a spirit of silver energy with a blue shimmer jumps up on the porch. It is a young girl, with long black hair. I think it is a girl. It has two sets of wings on its back—a cross between a fairy and a girl? She has the greenest eyes and a twinkling smile.

"Hi." She moves as if she can fly. I look again and there are no wings. But she is on the other side of the porch, sitting in a swing, legs crossed.

"Come to see Grandmother, have you? I know that shirt you wear. I know you've been on the river, chasing truth. Have you found it yet?"

"No, there's more need for growth."

"But before you see Grandmother Blue Star, let me add to your vision. It's the mountains and the sea gull that you seek, a place where the sea gull lives with the mountains. When you find this, there you place your impeccable flag. You'll know you're home where the sea gull meets the mountains."

She hops over backwards doing handsprings, and disappears into the woods. All kinds of laughter and giggling join her. It is as if the woods are alive with hundreds of children. Thousands of laughs ring through the woods. This place is alive and full of spirit—so inviting.

I continue walking. After a while the path grows dark. I seem to be lost. I come upon rocks and boulders, where I sit for a while. As I rest, I am distracted by tiny little yellow eyes peeking out from beneath the rocks. I feel frightened. I need to get back by the creek, to follow it back to the cabin, where I'll be able to find the teachings of Grandmother Blue Star.

Yellow eyes appear, disappear, then reappear. "Can any of you help me?" I ask. "I've lost my way. I need to get back to the creek, the one where the moon dance is, the one where I can walk the stones to Grandmother Blue Star's."

No one answers. Curiosity overwhelms me and I walk closer. Smoke comes from the rocks, a vapor. I begin to feel dizzy. The smoke has sounds in it that swirl around me. More yellow eyes appear in the rocks.

I walk further into the woods, feeling disillusioned. "I don't think I'm truly lost. I feel as if the river is not far from here." The forest is very mysterious. As I walk, the yellow eyes follow. It seems as if behind every tree and every rock there is a set of yellow eyes.

"Will you speak to me, you with yellow eyes? Will you tell me if I'm on the right track? Is this the path that I seek?"

I come to a clearing in the woods. I see mountains in the moonlight. A shadow passes in front of me across the trail. Many shadows pass in front of me, running quickly, darting here and there. I stop on the path. I am past feeling fear. Shadows are everywhere. Yellow eyes are watching. I decide I will run. I bolt through the woods, past the rocks to an open area where small creeks run. I stop by a boulder and lean against it. Off to the right are yellow eyes, but only one set this time. I hear a voice.

"Do you know what upheaval is? You probably have heard that curiosity killed the cat. That's a simple saying compared to upheaval."

I am face to face with the yellow eyes.

"If you know what entrapment is, then you can begin to understand upheaval."

I reply, "I think it's complicated, isn't it?"

Shadows dart all around me. I can feel things running through the woods, but the yellow eyes do not move.

"No. That's not the answer. Complicated is a different story. As you enter the woods, you seek the path of truth. On this path, feelings are your guides. People confuse feelings with emotions and they confuse emotions with feelings. In the spirit world, your feelings are your paths. To understand upheaval you need to understand your feelings and know them as pathways. These pathways then take you to passages. Through the passages you stand in truth.

"If you choose to follow the truth, then you are on the path of your vision. When you have followed your vision to its fullness, you then stand in gratitude. But before that can happen, you need to understand upheaval. This test lies before you now. You'll need all four stars to understand upheaval."

"I don't have my green star yet, I say. "So upheaval, for me, is not understanding growth."

"That's not what upheaval is," replies Yellow Eyes.

"Okay, then, are you—are you upheaval?"

"No. Remember what I told you a few moments ago."

I sit there on the rock, thinking.

"Maybe if I knew who you are, I'd have the answer to the question."

"If you knew me, entrapment would disappear. If you were to follow my medicine, you could face the bear and upheaval would never exist. If you knew my tracks, 'complicated' would no longer be a burden. Now, if you really knew me, you would know yourself. For long ago, before we were as we are now, curiosity killed us. We shifted and from that moment on we developed a species that knew. If you notice, I did not seek you out. You came upon my path. I was not advertising.

"As you walk your earth walk, what do you tell your students when they come in curiosity? What do you say to them when they're curious about the spirit way? What do you teach them when they look for the answers of upheaval?"

"I am a young teacher, I must find my green star, for growth is the answer to upheaval," I reply.

At that moment there is a loud, bellowing growl and out of the woods to the right of me steps a large grizzly bear. Its teeth are fierce, its eyes red. It is so enormous that I fall to the ground, shaking, frightened, and crawl behind the nearest tree. The bear stops and stares at me, its eyes intent.

"What do you say to your students? Answer the questions." The bear lifts its lips and snarls. Its large teeth sparkle in the moonlight.

I take a deep breath. "I ask them to face their disappointments. To look disappointment in the face and grow!"

The bear moves closer, its paws enormous, its eyes hard.

"Does that answer the questions inside? Does that strengthen them? Did that do any good for you when you had to face your disappointments? Deeper," the bear growls. "Go deeper. Your answers are not strong enough. Disappointment is destruction from within. Which is what I'll choose to do to you."

I turn to find Yellow Eyes, but it has disappeared. I am alone now with the bear, facing wrong answers and very large teeth. I try to draw on the strength of the knowledge that I am a wolf, but that truth isn't strong enough.

"Now do you know what upheaval is?" The bear comes one step closer. Behind him I see yellow eyes again. They are everywhere, watching, until finally the bear is totally surrounded by them. They peer out from behind the trees and rocks.

From a large rock beside me steps an enormous grey wolf with yellow eyes. It stands on its hind legs and faces the bear.

"This one comes to learn to be aware. This one will give me its full attention. Step back!"

The bear moves backward, one step at a time. The grey wolf, still on its hind legs, moves as a two-legged towards the bear.

"This one has come in knowing and now faces upheaval. To seek out the truth, this one will make commitment."

The enormous grizzly bellows, a howl that echoes through the woods, as it faces the grey wolf. They snort, snarl and growl. The bear takes a swing, and the wolf takes a swing. It seems that they are dancing in a circle, snarling, growling and slapping at each other. Fur flies. Yellow Eyes takes four swings, spins in a complete circle seven times, and the bear disappears. What remains is a silvery blue swirl of light where it had stood. This light settles to the ground.

The grey wolf turns and faces me. "Truth is your path. It lies before you."

There in the moonlight shimmers a blue path.

"There's your path, through the pines to the river. Walk on now. We, the yellow eyes, are your family. We watch. You're never alone in the pack. The grey wolf stands at the edge and listens. The multi-colored ones simply are, so that you might be."

Yellow Eyes nods up and down, motioning towards the path. I begin to walk. I feel carefree and young. The morning has begun. The dawn of light lies before me. As I step away from Yellow Eyes, I hear, "Devotion. The path that you seek to Blue Star is devotion. Remember to be devoted."

I step into the morning light as the sun begins to rise. The path becomes easy. Up ahead of me is Grandmother's cabin, with familiar smoke and the river that runs past the back. I run quickly and jump to the porch. I smell the coffee. I step through the door and there to greet me is an older woman with a familiar face, and blue stars for eyes.

"Your walk through the woods, did you like it?" she asks.

"Oh, Grandmother, I learned a lot of things. I learned about feelings. Most mysterious, though, is the word devotion. The need to be devoted. I seek out the truth, Grandmother Blue Star. The truth of memory, the most ancient medicine of all. Knowing that as you place your foot, it has been and always will be."

"Sit. We haven't long. We must prepare to meet the truth."

I sit down at the familiar kitchen table, by the back door, and watch the river. I love that feeling of watching water rush past the back door.

"It's easy to get disillusioned. It's easy to entrap yourself. Entrapment happens when one detaches from one's purpose. We have more to do than gaze at the river. We have more to do than sit at a familiar table. You must go with me. We must perform the ceremony of truth where you will receive your blue star. Then on, to seek out wisdom. To understand the truth of the purple star."

"But, Grandmother, I don't have my green star. I'm concerned about the green star."

Her steel-blue eyes cut to me sharply. "Asking questions is not the truth. Remember, you must *know* to truly have the green star. To stand in the realm of impeccability, you must know. Here in the spirit world we have a short time to prepare you."

Grandmother Blue Star instructs me to gather my thoughts together.

I feel a strong spirit around me, as if I am being watched. I turn, and there are those dark eyes. He looks at me with depth and an inviting smile.

"Your quest for the truth is at hand. Today is the ceremony of truth. You will earn your blue star," he says as he joins me at the table.

"I had a most unusual experience trying to find my way back. I came across a very large bear whose personality overwhelmed me."

He looks at me with a distance in his eyes. "I don't think it is as much the personality of the bear as it is your lack of truth."

He draws a cup of coffee and sips on it slowly. "You concentrate on the fear of not knowing your green star. Today is the ceremony of truth, so you'll know. You'll understand that the green light is always. Most speak of it as growth, but that's the aftermath. It's before that when the green star is needed."

His voice has a growl to it. "When Grandmother Blue Star takes you for your ceremony of truth, you will also encounter Grandmother Purple Star. Then you will stand in the circle of elders where Rainbow Medicine will be a reality. This journey that lies ahead of you is only possible when faith is in your heart. I have come this time to show you faith. Do you wish the totality of your vision?" he asks. "If so, you must leave these familiar surroundings and take on your vision. The truth is, nothing is always. And we are not together," he says, crossing his fingers one over the other. "And we are together," as he holds his fingers apart.

"To have true bear medicine, to know what is within, you must understand what I say."

I feel a loneliness when he shows me this. I feel small and inadequate. He reaches over, touches my chin and lifts my head.

"You see what I mean? Faith is necessary here. It's beyond the realm of the physical. You teach the way of individuality as you walk as a two-legged.

All you have to do is sit and teach. It sounds so simple. And where simplicity is, so is faith."

I know that when I turn, he will be gone. I am beginning to understand what faith is. I gather up my medicine robe and bundle, and walk out the door. I step off the porch of the familiar cabin and walk away down the path. I hear a whisper from the woods.

"No one said you have to forget. No one said you have to let go. Remember. Understand what commitment is. Here, on the path of the blue star, commitment is uppermost. It is the connection to reality. When it is lost, there is only insanity, distortion, lack of faith. Today is your ceremony of truth. Remember," the wind whispers. "Remember. Commitment. And most of all, devotion. To be devoted."

Wind swirls through the pines. Ahead I see Grandmother Blue Star standing with her bundle and two horses. I think this will be a test of devotion to commitment. And then I remember I am spirit. I needn't worry about physical failure, inadequacy or a lesson maybe forgotten. The old woman mounts the horse swiftly. I join her and we ride like the wind.

Through the trees we weave our way, far into the day as the sun rises and then begins to sink downwards. As night descends, we come to a passage. Grandmother does not tire or falter. I will always remember her endurance, and the long hours that we travel when she speaks no words. As we enter the passage she stops and her horse drops its head. Mine stands beside it. Their noses touch and they both disappear. We now stand beside each other.

The passage before me is grey stone. Through it I see a dark presence, awesome, foreboding. And within it is an even darker color—deeper, richer, the darkest shade of dark I have ever experienced. The passage goes on before us. As we step in, I realize the darkness is just a deeper shade of blue. Grandmother Blue Star speaks.

"Your fear is only a deeper shade of blue," and she laughs. "Things within truth are always rich. There is a tremendous amount of wealth and you must remember this about the deeper shade of blue. Now you are in the place of ceremony."

I Hear the Rapid Beat of the Drum Calling Me Back.

Rainbow Medicine

Story Doll—the Truth Teller

Needed: *Pine cones; branches with leaves; hot glue gun; small sticks; 11 colors of string; red 100% cotton cloth; skin pieces; feathers; buttons; pins*

The story doll is built by collecting objects that have meaning and tell the story of your life. Build your doll as you want, to speak your truth to you.

Example: I built my body from a pine cone for growth and everlasting life. I used small strong oak twigs for strength and a crystal for a head, which I glued to the pine cone. I used crystal for clear thinking. I placed wolf fur on the cone for my inner self—the wolf.

Place your doll so you can see and hear the story of your self.

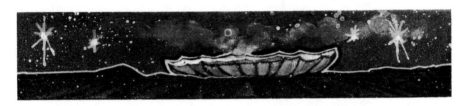

The Ceremony to Find Truth

Tools: *Rocks or cornmeal; journal and pen; bowl of tobacco*

1. **A vision of respect.** Go to your safest place, a place that has no memories of pain or abuse. A place where you and only you are present with Great Spirit. There, set a sacred circle (page 43) by drawing it in the ground or building it with rocks or cornmeal. Stand on the outside of the circle. Take four deep breaths, in through your nose and out through your mouth.

   Look in the circle and allow yourself to have a vision that brings forth for you the symbol for respect. See it and hold it in your mind.

   > *Example:* I see four blue stars. I bring them back and put them in my journal. As I record the first star, I hear the word "commit." With the second star, I hear the word "discipline." For the third star, I hear the word "understanding" and for the fourth star I hear "limitless."

   After you have recorded the symbols that you receive, journal the feelings that you have about them.

   Still outside the circle, look around. This outside area represents "misdirected." Think for a moment of the many times you have been misdirected, when you've missed the mark, when it's not been so for you. Journal some of those times.

Now step inside the circle of respect. Raise your arms high unto Father Sky and give to Grandfather and Grandmother Spirit your promise of truth. Remember the symbol for respect that has been given to you, and walk towards the belief that is truth for you.

2. **A vision of honor.** Sit in the circle, a bowl of tobacco in front of you. Take four deep breaths in through your nose and out through your mouth, and relax. Draw a trail in front of you, from left to right, with the tobacco. As you do this, see another symbol—a symbol for honor.

> *Example:* As I lay the tobacco trail, I see seven wolf tracks. I journal this and, as I do, I hear the words "confidence, balance, creativity, growth, truth, wisdom, impeccability." From this symbol of the wolf tracks, I find my honor.

After you have recorded your vision, your symbol, and listened for the words of interpretation, hold a bit of tobacco in your hand, lifting it up to Great Spirit. Thank Great Spirit for your honor. Give tobacco to Mother Earth, and thank Mother Earth for your honor. Give tobacco to the East, and give thanks for illumination. And to the South, give thanks for the growth that lies ahead. To the West, give thanks for the understanding that you'll walk with, and to the North, give thanks for the wisdom that you will gain. Hold the tobacco to your heart and accept your truth, which is your honor.

Recall the times that you have been disillusioned. Think about the times you have distrusted, been misguided or misdirected. Journal these experiences. From your respect and honor, and your personal connection with the four directions, Great Spirit and Mother Earth, let go of this disillusionment. Turn away from the disillusion, the addictions, the abuses, the misguided actions and feelings that you carry that bring disrespect to your elders and to yourself. Remember what you have been given as symbols of honor and of respect.

3. **A vision of sacred.** Using stones, build a tight circle as close to you as possible. Take four breaths and begin to vision your symbol of sacred—what is sacred to you.

> *Example:* I see a red ruby, a green emerald, a blue lapis and a brilliant crystal. I journal this and, as I do, I hear the words "family, knowing, tomorrow, excitement, fulfillment."

Journal your feelings about the word "sacred," your symbol for sacredness, the vision you have received. Write your interpretation of these things. When you have finished, look at each one of the stones that have tightened around you. Journal the things that have entrapped you, things that have taken your time, that are not good for you, that do not happen in a good way—things that have separated you from your sacred self.

Begin to see these things being replaced by what is sacred, what brings you honor and respect. Recall the symbols for respect and honor and sacredness. Connect at this moment with the good lessons that you have received and build upon what is sacred to you in your mind. Journal this.

4. **A vision of enlightenment.** Take four deep breaths in and out. Vision your symbol for enlightenment.

> *Example:* I see a very bright silvery-white light totally engulfing me. I journal this as my obedience to Creator's love, the knowledge of my totality, my ability to create.

Journal your feelings around your vision of enlightenment. Then think about the things that disappoint you or bring disappointment into your life and journal these feelings. Now replace them with your vision of enlightenment, knowing what is sacred to you, what brings you honor and respect.

5. **A vision of faith.** Stand and walk to the edge of your circle. Stand right on the line so that you are in and out at the same time. Take four deep breaths. There you will see your symbol for faith.

> *Example:* I'm standing on a cliff. Before me all I see is sky. Interpretation: It's my path. I can jump or stay. A solid knowing turns me around.

Journal your feelings of faith. Then list the things that bring upheaval to you, things that push you past your lines, past your principles—things that you cannot control but which control you—dependencies that you bend under. Now replace these with your symbol for faith, of being enlightened, knowing that you are sacred, bringing honor and respect to yourself. Remember the visions and symbols that you have been given.

6. **A vision of simplicity.** Step out of the circle and walk around it four times clockwise. During the fourth time around, look into the circle and find your vision or symbol for what is simple.

Example: Finishing the fourth round, I look into the wheel and see seven marbles of seven colors. Interpretation as I journal: Life is as it is for a child. Everything can be played, put away and done again tomorrow.

When you have journalled your vision of simplicity, list the things that are complicated to you—the things that tear away your truth, your peace of mind, your individuality. Replace them with the symbol for what is simple. Apply your symbols for faith, enlightenment, sacredness, honor and respect.

7. **A vision of truth.** Walk a distance away from your circle. Turn back, look at your circle and see your symbol for truth.

   Example: I walk a good 44 paces away, turn and look back to my circle. There I see a rushing waterfall with a faint rainbow crossing it. Interpretation: The energy of the teachings are my truth. Through and behind the rainbow is mystery. The unknown becomes known.

8. **Things you are curious about.** When you have received your symbol and journalled the interpretation, list the things that you are curious about—all the unknowns, all the things that you want to know more about. Replace them with your symbol for truth, knowing that things are simple if you have faith. If you are enlightened, then all is sacred and the symbol for honor is with you. You have the respect of truth.

Aho.

· 13 ·
The Purple Star

I breathe in and out gently, four times. Before me, a familiar path takes me into an open field and a very dark night. I see four shooting stars, their tails streamers of iridescent blue. I think of the blue stars and memories of dark eyes. The feeling of love warms me. My truth, I hold in my heart—the blue star. I know that I have respect. I have felt the feelings of sacredness.

In the night I stand, with no emptiness. I hold the memories of Grandmother Blue Star, her strength and fortitude. But now I must find the purple star. My memories of confidence, balance and creativity unfold the path before me. I am committed to this path. I know the sun, the red star, the orange star, the yellow star, and I hold their symbols within me. I will have the totality of the green star, faith. I understand the depth of introspection, that life is very simple. This is truth for me. I hold the blue star as a reality, that the simple way through life is downstream.

"That's right," a soft voice whispers. "Which way do you go when the river is rough? Do you know how to ask a question? How will you find your purple star, if you don't know how to ask a question?"

I look around. Nothing is there but darkness, the wind and blades of grass, stalks of wheat. Ahead of me is a very old oak, barren of leaves. It seems dead. I begin to walk towards the tree.

"Hello?" I call out. "Is anyone here at this old tree?"

There is a stillness, so cold that it shakes my heart. I look on the other side of the tree, and there is a grave. I see no mark on the stone. Clouds fill the sky and behind them shines an enormous full moon. The clouds drift across the moon and a cold wind blows.

"Do you know how to ask a question?"

I stand there, in mystery. I search deep inside of me. "If I say yes, that would be an answer," I reply. "How do I ask a question . . . is a question."

"Right, so you must know how to ask a question. Do not tease about the search for knowledge. Do not act dumb when looking for the questions. Do not act as if you don't know, for this is not confidence. When confidence is gone, you have lost your balance. Creativity consists of the energy of all that is balanced and confident. There is no hope for growth without creation. Do you know how to ask the question? This is the truth, and from it will come the purple star."

"Hoot, hoot," calls an owl. I turn, seeking the owl, and a dark shadow passes in front of me. There beside the tree stands the shape of a woman, yet I can see horns. A dark purple mist swirls around the tree, engulfing the figure. The clouds move from the moon, illuminating a female—her hair jet black, her eyes piercing. Only one eye, I see. She turns her head and I see a large screech owl's face, a yellow eye. No, the shadow shifts—a great horned owl, a snowy white. It moves and disappears into the mist.

"Now do you know the question?"

The voice calls from behind me. I spin around, face-to-face with that half-owl, half-woman.

"No. She doesn't."

From behind me a stronger voice, but feminine. I turn, and there stands another woman in a white fox cape. She is all in purple lace, satin and silk—the finest of cloths. She wears a beautiful amethyst necklace, pale and dark purple. Her purple eyes dance with a lightning bolt of yellow in the center.

"You will have the cleverness to answer the question of One Eye."

The owl woman lifts its wing, covers its face, turns and screeches. "Sherk!" Then it scurries into the dark.

I look back at the woman in fox. Moonlight hits her eyes, showing purple stars that glisten. A lavender fog swirls around me and I become very dizzy, very heavy, very tired. I lie down on the grave. My fear dissipates and I hug the grave.

144 *Rainbow Medicine*

"I am the one you seek, Grandmother Purple Star. I am the keeper of ancient wisdom. The one who removes karma."

She kneels beside me. I look at her face and see the woman that is there behind the fox. Her hair is white, yet red. There is fire in her eyes, yet they are dull. She is something I am, something that is similar to me.

"Yes," she says. "You are more when you pull from the wisdom within. When you truly walk with bear medicine, you reach deep inside the pool of truth. In that pool is what wisdom is about. Come with me."

Like a shot of light she takes off, zigzagging across the land. I run behind her. At first I feel I can't keep up. Then a bolt of energy from the wolf overtakes my two-legged's mind and I begin to leap and lope, zipping through the field with the speed of the wind. I stop beside the woman. Her eyes dance with a silvery shimmer of purple. Her eyes are clouds.

I go into the clouds. Sparkles of light flicker and bounce off each other— a misty, pale purple, shimmering silver, white—so white it is blue. I feel clean and fresh.

"Where am I?" echoes through the clouds.

"In the mind of wisdom. You are inside Grandmother Purple Star, Grandmother Wisdom. In the North realm of the wheel in the winter. In the dead of night, long after one o'clock in the morning. The spirit of renewal is wisdom; it has the depth of power. Where pure is home—this is where you are."

I see a field of snow, deep, cold, glistening in the moonlight. In the middle of the field is a fire circle with benches made of cut rounds from trees. I see some figures standing as the dancing flames climb high. Around the fire circle is a beaten path that looks as if it has been danced away.

"Where is this, and what is this, Grandmother?"

A sizzle sound swishes past me.

"This is the circle of realness. It is within power, within wisdom, that you are standing. You will come here and you will listen quietly to what is spoken by the Council of Elders. You will hear the seven sacred teachings, revealed in their totality within your vision. You will remember."

As I walk closer to the council, I notice Grandfather Red Star, Grandfather Orange Star, and Grandfather Yellow Star. Grandmother Green Star, Grandmother Blue Star, and Grandmother Purple Star. And there, Grandmother Burgundy Star. And there are other stars, other spirits of energy. I walk through many shimmering, glimmering energies and they part as I pass. I notice the footprints of a wolf coming out from the circle.

I hear the elders speaking. From Grandmother Blue Star, "Here within the Circle of Wisdom, the Council of Reality, we speak the need that all two-leggeds understand the Great School of Mystery known as life. It is time that obedience is understood. For those who seek the white light, the rainbow path, the good Red Road, it is time to reconnect and kindle impeccability. The teacher of impeccability, of the ways of the absolute, walks this rainbow path, the path of respect, and leaves footprints for others to find their way home."

Grandmother Purple Star motions for me to stand next to her. I step between her and Grandmother Burgundy Star. I sneak a look at Grandmother Burgundy Star out of the corner of my eye, for there is great mystery there. I see the face of a white wolf and, in the eyes, I see myself. It is a frightening feeling. I quickly look back into the fire and I see the large white wolf looking back at me, smiling with its eyes.

Grandmother Purple Star asks if I know what wisdom is. If I will speak it in the presence of the elders of knowledge. I gaze at the fire and draw strength from the white wolf in my heart and begin to speak.

"Wisdom is the ability to look within the fire and see yourself. In that is the confidence that Grandfather Red Star has given me.

"The ways of wisdom are Balance, as Grandfather Orange Star has taught me. When fear is in balance, ceremony is at hand, and flow is there. Grandfather Yellow Star has taught the need for creativity that brings forth Great Spirit's teachings. These are the wisdoms that I have learned within this council, that I have been given in my vision of the sun and the stars and the moon.

"The aloofness of Grandmother Green Star allows me to have faith that someday I'll understand what the true quest for growth is all about. This is the greatest wisdom of all. It allows me to experience truth—a truth, my truth, their truth, the truth. I dance around with these words in my heart. I go to the ceremony of truth with respect and humbleness. As I study from Grandmother Truth, I feel that seeing is believing. See it in your life and it is so.

"Looking into your eyes, Grandmother Wisdom, I see that the shamanic way, the Rainbow Path, the connection with the Great What Is— Grandfather Spirit—is eternal movement, the constant search for the green star that enables us to grow beyond each day, to have direction and open a path to the stars. As I hear the elders speak in my vision, when you reach for the stars you heal the scars.

"I look towards impeccability for the answers of my vision, the way to use wisdom to heal the scars. I have absolute confidence that all is well and good, deeply secure and connected. I attribute that to knowing."

I feel very humble. A voice speaks.

"You are these voices of the seven sacred teachings, and in your heart are the words of the elders. The celebration of life and experience that you have

146 *Rainbow Medicine*

gained in this is all yours. You seek the spirit within, the true shaman within, that plays its drum in the beat of your heart. You hold within you the answers of each heartbeat that connects with the eternal heartbeat of Great Spirit."

At that moment they disappear. I stand alone in a field of snow, listening to the heartbeat, listening to the drum, the connecting beat of constant life.

I turn. The owl woman is watching me with a faraway look in her eye. She disappears into a shadow, but as she flies past, she drops a feather that floats to my feet. I look at the owl and the thought of death crosses my mind. I look up, and there stands a skeleton.

"Why have you come?" I ask.

"To remind you of the way. To remind you that nothing stays the same. Consistency is constant change. How can you find comfort in constant change? I call you to the bone people. I ask that you be a hollow bone. I ask that you watch, always, the movement of wisdom."

The skeleton turns around and as it walks away I see the tail of the fox swishing back and forth. That crafty, clever old grandmother! I bend to pick up the owl feather but it is gone.

It's night and there's a full moon around me. I remember the teachings of Purple Star. I follow the path as it works its way into the mountains and soon find myself at the top, on a thin, rocky trail that looks out into the valley below. I work my way along, anticipating the next star.

My foot slips and I begin to fall. I grab a little rock that's hanging out and hold on. Whew! I pull myself back up and I'm on the trail again. Standing in front of me is a dark, tense spirit—part raven, part man.

"This is the path of the void. Follow it carefully, for the void is to your left. To your right is the mountain. The symbolism that lies here is yours to interpret. Speak of what you know."

I am taken by the raven, its huge size, strength and intensity. Eyes as deep and vast as the void to my left. Feathers so dark the colors shimmer, concealed within the black.

"I'll interpret," I answer. "To my right is the mountain, which is my wisdom, my solidity. To my left is the void, absence, rejection. Why are you here?"

The raven caws four times. "Why you have come is why I am here. What do you seek from the burgundy star? I am the spirit keeper. I am the one who guards the sacred, precious teachings of all spirit knowledge. To confront the raven is to confront magic. If you cannot interpret natural occurrences, you cannot know the depth of wisdom or impeccability. You're encountering the judge of spirit, the one who sees whether you endure the teachings of the wolf. The wolf is the way, the one who knows, the one who leads the path to Grandfather/Grandmother Great Spirit. There all color is, and all is fair and good, rich and real. Why have you come seeking this path of Rainbow Medicine?"

I take a deep breath and relax. I remember the stones that I hold in my medicine pouch. "Confidence is what I seek, and I have that. The balance of life and death. The need for appreciation. There are many reasons, but most of all it is because my vision has called me. I have seen the sun and the moon and the seven stars and it is my job to answer the questions of the weary. Only from the vision can I find that truth, Raven."

"Caw. Caw." He flies high, soaring out over the left, over the void, and disappears.

I pass where the Raven stood. As I walk along the thin ledge in the moonlight, I think of judgment—of the wrongs and the rights that I have learned as a two-legged. The path becomes so narrow I can barely put one foot in front of the other. A feeling of crushing pressure comes over me. It is hard to keep moving, but I know that this, too, is a judgment.

I am very dizzy, very sleepy but there is no place to lie down, just this thin walkway. My eyes close.

I awake next to a warm fire. There is a small table with a warm cup of tea next to me. I am wrapped in a purple striped medicine blanket, looking into the eyes of Grandmother Purple Star.

"Wisdom is knowing where you are all of the time. It's having the ability to use your vision as your medicine. What is your vision? That is your wisdom. Wisdom is similar to balance. It is, it isn't. It can be, it won't be. It might be, it should be. As you put in confidence, balance comes out— then creativity. By then your growth soars. You experience things from many different angles and it's exciting. Remember this."

I Hear the Rapid Beat of the Drum Calling Me Back.

Hair Tie

Needed: *A piece of red 100% cotton cloth cut 16 inches (40cm) long and one-half inch (1.25cm) wide; colored beads*

As you cut the cloth for your hair tie, think of the commitment you wish to make. When you have the hair tie cut, braid it into your hair at the back of your head where it will hang over your left shoulder. Then tie on beads at the end of the tie. These beads will represent the medicine you will use to fulfill your commitment.

> *Example:* I cut my hair tie to wear during a powwow in honor of my mother's illness. I placed blue beads for truth, purple beads for wisdom to understand and white beads to know Great Spirit is with me.

It is very important to know that a hair tie is a way of honor. The hair tie is not for a party or dress-up, but a way of showing the lessons you are learning. Or of showing respect of people in your life. It is the way with all objects worn in the hair—animal skin or feathers, shells and beads, cloth—everything worn in the hair is a piece of honor and respect, lessons learned.

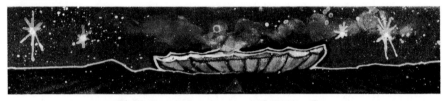

The Ceremony of Wisdom

Tools: *4 white feathers or symbols of them; stick; journal and pen; tobacco or cornmeal*

Within the ceremony of wisdom I would first ask that you place this statement within your journal:

> As I choose to become wise, I address the elders of the sacred teachings of Grandfather Spirit. I ask that they bless me with the humbleness to give to all my relations everything that I am. I call for wisdom, and am responsible for understanding that I will be working with the energy of growth, that Grandmother Green Star will be with me. That the flow must be. I am responsible for understanding that wisdom goes downstream. If I should fight and want to swim upstream, I would be going against my faith, by fighting wisdom instead of going with the flow. I will be responsible for the learning that comes to me as I call for my wisdom.

The four white feathers may be from turkey or chicken. They represent owl feathers. Understand that through the power of individuality a symbol can be anything. It can be cut from paper or cardboard. Realize that we don't need to buy, or cheat, or steal to have objects that are only symbols. If we are gifted by the winged ones, then we are fortunate to have our eagle feathers, owl feathers, hawk feathers. But in respect of our elders, the indigenous people of Native American legacies and blood, we are not to disrespect by killing, stealing, buying, lying or cheating to obtain feathers.

There are four steps in the ceremony of wisdom:

1. **Understanding.** Go to the woods alone, in the night. Seek the right spot by feeling and listening to the energy flowing in and around you. Pick the spot that brings up the most fears: defeat, deceit, confusion, anger, disconnection, or that something is there, watching you—that it could get you.

   Once you have felt that spot, stand very still and hold a feather in your hand. Place the feather in front of your eyes and look through it. You will begin to see as an owl sees, all the way around you. You'll be able to see very clearly everything that moves in the woods. Understanding is at hand now. Breathe in and out four times, and walk into the area of deceit, the place where you have deceived yourself and given away your power.

   As you walk into this area, see it becoming well lit by bright light coming from the Creator in your spirit. Feel your deceit begin to weaken. Walk this area in a clockwise direction, thinking about what has weakened you in your life, what has taken your understanding away—how you have given your power to the evils of others. How you fear rape and murder, being beaten, being over-ridden by others' feelings and power. As you walk this area, deal with denial, say to yourself, "I probably have weaknesses. I have many. I give those to this deceit and I let go now. I choose not to defy or to deny. I choose not to deceive myself, but to know that I am a powerless two-legged who draws its spirit and power from Great Spirit, Creator."

   Walk this area four full times, then stop, open your eyes, and feel the energy of Great Spirit all around you. Find the center of this area, and stick the feather in the ground. Step back four feet from the feather, and draw a circle around it. Stand on the outside of that circle and look at the feather in the ground. As you look at it, you will be given a symbol for understanding. See it very clearly in your mind and remember it. It is the medicine that you need to understand, the medicine that it takes to defeat disillusion and disconnection. It is the first step in understanding wisdom. All your fears are to be understood.

2. **Power.** Sit very close to the circle, on the outside. Think of the most powerful things that you know.

   Examples: waterfalls, wind storms, hurricanes, tornadoes. The power of Great Spirit and of the elemental people, the thunder beings, the lightning people, the spirit walkers of the great sky people, the grand power of the elemental clans: fire, wind, earth, water.

Come to an understanding of what true power is.

List in your journal the powers that have taken your power away.

Example: Someone else's control, a codependent relationship, deceit that has led you astray, a denial of your own capability, the physical and mental abuse of another. List the things that you have given power to.

When you see these areas, draw from yourself the energy to know, to have your answers before you. Understand that true power is spiritual and not physical. As you compare the power of the spirit world and elementals to the places that have felt powerful to you, go to the core of understanding what true power is. Ask yourself why things happen. Find the reasoning in "why," and claim those reasons for yourself, understanding your need of them, understanding their purpose in your life.

3. **Respect.** Step inside the circle. Take from your medicine bundle your tobacco or cornmeal and give respect to the earth by placing either on the ground. As you give this, ask for the ability to understand what true respect is and hear words of respect come into your mind. Understand that when respect is at hand, it is an action of giving from yourself to another. It is a give-away of your need and a return of what is necessary. Having respect opens the doorway to the mental plane and expands your wisdom so that you may truly walk the path of the wolf and find what is home for yourself.

The third teaching of wisdom. See each color and connect a medicine word to it: red for confidence, orange for balance, and so on. Understand that to have power, respect must be at hand. These avenues of wisdom allow you to succeed in your two-legged walk and to have a healthy spirit.

4. **Knowing.** Moving into the position to the North, stand and look back at the circle. In the center of the circle you'll see the owl feather. See an owl in your mind and connect this image to the feather, whether the feather is artificial or not or even specifically from a different bird. In honor of the owl, reflect on what you have placed in the center.

Think about deceit now. Illusion or disillusion. Magic is illusion—magical thinking is not a truly natural flow. Disillusion is a trick. To deceive is only one side of reality.

Then think about wisdom—the ability to know, to understand things, to respect.

- CONFIDENCE: Walk around the outside of the circle once and stand at the spot where you started. Think back now on what it takes to be confident. Journal your feelings of confidence. Look for any fears that may be covering up your confidence. List them in your journal. Allow the fears to go. Stand in your confidence.
- BALANCE: Now step to the left and walk around the wheel again. Stop. The balance of owl medicine is that there are two sides always, the good and the bad. Look at the good and bad in your life. List them. Ask yourself who taught you the good and the bad. Ask yourself what is so for you. Find the wisdom in good and the wisdom in bad. Choose what is so for you.
- CREATIVITY: Again, take one step to the left and walk around the circle. Stop. Now look at the creativity of the owl. The ability— which is wisdom—and the lie, which is deceit. We've been taught that lying is a bad thing. Go to the core of the word "lie." What motivates your lies? To fit in? To be a part of? To be as good as? To have what someone else is—to be like someone else? What motivates your lies is the disease within your life, the disconnectedness. It comes from the feeling that you are not enough, that you need to fit together. Find the creative way out of deceit.
- GROWTH: Step clockwise and move around the circle again. Stop. Look back at the owl and see growth, where your life has taken you. See yourself knowing, being organized, confident and patient, having harmony, direction and creativity. Then see your deceit, your feelings of inadequacy. List these feelings and examine what you feel you're not. Where is the anger, the fear, the sadness? List these things.
- TRUTH: Step clockwise and go around again. Stop. Look at the owl feather and think of the truth. What is the truth of knowing? How do you ever know? Look at your deceit, knowing nothing, feeling empty or ignorant or not good enough.

Take a deep breath at this point, and let it out easy. Do this four times and allow yourself to be with what you know. Make a list of the things that you do not know. Ask yourself if you want the answers to these truths and are willing to walk the path to accept them. Look at knowing: that you are you and you have no right to step into another's circle. That imposing yourself on another is not true for you. To step into deceit, to control and manipulate, to lie, to have what is not yours because it has not been given—all of this is not yours. Accept these things for what they are. Breathe in your truth. What is your path? How do you complete your walk?

- WISDOM: Step clockwise and move around the circle. Stop. Look at the feather and the owl's life from wisdom, from the movement of knowing. List the places in your life where you feel you have given up your faith, given up your hope, let yourself down, not been able to expand into a realm that is truth. List the things that have deceived you, that you have given your power to, that you feel you have permitted to take away your wisdom.

- IMPECCABILITY: Step clockwise and go around the circle, stopping next to where you originally began. Look at the owl feather and see impeccability, a correct way, a pure way. Wisdom is understanding that you're always forgiven. That everything is okay. That each of us has individuality and when you're not a part of someone's space, you belong someplace else. Feel the importance of that, the absoluteness. Feel this reflecting your knowledge of your path. Know that you never need to cling, or cry or plead out of fear or deceit. You never need to deceive the self, but be straight up with your confidence, knowing that you will find where you belong, that you have the creativity to create your space.

- CLOSING: Now walk around the circle and give cornmeal or tobacco out of thanks for knowing, for having the ability to walk in the space of wisdom. As you come back to where you started, draw four breaths in and out in honor of the directions. Place a white feather at each point of direction in the circle.

> The first breath and feather is to the East. To have wisdom there must be a beginning, and that is understanding.
> The second breath and feather is to the South, for the actuality, the growth. This is the power, the ability to do.
> The next breath and feather is to the West. Movement, the physical, the being. This is the respect.
> The fourth breath and feather is to the North. The ongoing, the outcome, wisdom itself. And this is knowing.

Step into the circle now and face yourself and your fears. Do this by looking and remembering that you have placed the wisdom feather in each direction. You have the medicine of wisdom to carry with you in the days that lie ahead on the path of your earth walk.

Aho.

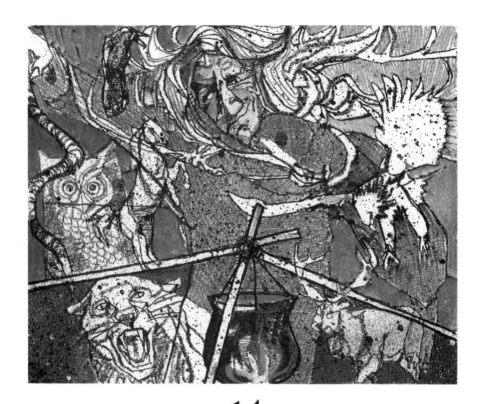

· 14 ·

The Burgundy Star

I gently breathe in and out. Before me I see a road, up ahead an ordinary cattle gate. Spring is around me. I see dogwood trees mixed in among all the green, new birth leaves. I walk up the road towards the gate. There is a memory inside of me of absence—an abandoned feeling.

An intense loneliness comes over me, but I've reached the gate now. On it is a very small sign that says "Heaven." Inside my mind I smile. I feel as if I'm in two places at once. As I open the gate and step within, there is cold air around me and a familiar smell of Nature welcoming. I walk ahead. A small stream rushes past me—gentle water rippling over the rocks.

I stop and sit on a rock, watching the water rush past me. There is a quietness in my heart here. It feels like home—no stress, no worries, no fear. Maybe this really is heaven.

Across the creek, a beautiful woman with intense eyes is looking at me.

"You have a choice, always. As did your ancestors. No one takes away your choice."

"Can you tell me where I am?" I ask her. "In heaven?"

"Not on my side of the water," she replies. "There is no place."

Like home? "There is no place like home" echoes in my mind.

"I'm in search of two stars. The fullness of the green star and the teaching of the burgundy star. Do you know anything about these teachings or about this vision I have?"

"Crossing the river is what I know about," she replies, a dullness in her voice. "A choice is made and once you have crossed the river the choice becomes change. The ceremony has taken place. You find your own vision, here in this land." I see Dark-Eyes with her, holding her hand.

They disappear in a pale grey mist. I feel as if everything I know that matters to me has been stripped away. Everything that I am is gone. As I continue walking I listen to the winged ones around me singing their sweet song of day. I cross a field of yellow flowers to get to a small waterfall. The water is deep, clear and cool. Each drop sings to me of long-ago memories as it falls in the pond.

I decide to camp and gather rocks to build a circle. I gather wood to build a fire as the evening comes and place my roll where I can sleep. I lie on the ground and stare at the stars. I feel myself dozing as the stars become bright in the night. Wind swirls around me. The swish of a tail passes by.

I wake looking into the face of Dark-Eyes. On his finger he wears a ring, round and dark.

"I have met you once before. Our paths cross in a good way, I hope."

He looks at me intently. "Do you understand the green star yet? Have you obtained the lesson of growth?"

"I'm not sure," I reply.

He shifts in the moonlight and looks at me sharply. "You have no control, or need for control, in the spirit world. All is yours to pull from and to know. The lessons are peace—they are yours to hold and to walk with. From the edge I watch you struggle and seek your control. Speak to me of your vision. Tell me what you know."

He places wood on the fire, which dances its strength. Through the fire a dragon appears, with wings, piercing red eyes and forked tongue.

"I see a dragon behind you, don't I?"

He looks at me and says, "Speak of your vision. The keeper of the fire is always here."

"My vision has called me and I have followed it. Through the sacred doors of the sun, knowledge has been revealed. By seeking out the red star I have found confidence. The orange star is balance. The yellow star is creativity. The green star is growth."

I stop for a moment. "I still seek the answers to growth. The blue star is truth. The purple star is wisdom. And now I stand in the teachings of the burgundy star."

He shifts and disappears in the smoke. All that is left is the dragon. Slowly, it fades in the fire. I feel tired and very alone. I rest in the loneliness and feel its depth pull me. I cover myself with its emptiness.

"Call me and I'll come. Name me, and I'll be there," I hear his voice in the wind.

"I only know you as Dark-Eyes, and you play with my feelings. You're a tempter and a tester. Do you want something from me? Why else would you leave me with such an empty feeling?" Sleep becomes my friend and I rest in the night.

Morning comes and the fire has died. Spring has turned to hot summer.

From down the road I hear, "Come. Come to me. I'll answer your questions of the burgundy star. I'll take you on the ridge to meet Grandmother Wolf. I believe you would call her Grandmother Burgundy Star. But first, you must have your vision, your heart's calling. Come with me."

I know better than to go with Dark-Eyes. I know it would just be another round where I would be left feeling empty. The games are getting old now, but yet . . . something calls me forward to follow him. I watch him run along the rock beside the creek, swift as a winged one. I follow as fast as I can. We travel long and far back into the woods, along the ridges. We come to a breathtaking view that looks out over the crests of the mountains.

"A scene I paint for you, like music." He runs ahead of me with youthful bounds. "Follow me. I'll take you to the gate of Grandmother's home."

I wonder how he knows the Grandfathers and Grandmothers and their stories. The heat of the day is around me and I walk along slowly, watching the river run beside the woods. It laces its way through the pines. Dark-Eyes has disappeared ahead of me. I come around a tree and there on the ground lies a beautiful buffalo robe. A soft cool breeze wafts through the trees. This feels good, a place to rest.

I lie on the buffalo robe. The trees here are withered, twisted and very old. Before me appears an enormous elk. "I am stamina. I am endurance. You must pass through me to find the burgundy star. You must know my story."

A need to be loved and to love comes over me. The elk struts around me and my heart begins to pound. From behind the tree Dark-Eyes appears, a long braid down his back. On his bare chest hangs a tooth that I cannot recognize. He extends his hand and I feel myself disappear in his eyes. I become one with his heartbeat. I am entangled in the love that he gives so freely. Behind him I see the elk, with enormous horns. The world begins to spin. I lose track of time. I am engulfed in his physicality.

"Give me your most precious thing."

I wake on the robe to these words. Dark-Eyes is nowhere in sight. The summer has turned to fall. It starts to rain and the buffalo robe is gone. I sit there in the mountains, watching autumn come in. I remember what a teacher once said to me: "Don't hold on to the vision. Don't force it. Don't try to make it happen. Let it flow."

With that, I let go, and before me stands an old woman with a cane and a burgundy blanket shawl. I cannot see her face clearly, but I can see her crooked, spiral-shaped cane. She stands in a natural archway in the pines. On each side of her stands a coyote. She motions with her cane and an enormous raven flies in front of her and lands on her shoulder. It takes flight again, circling me, crying, "Caw. Caw."

The old woman turns and walks back into the thicket of trees. I follow. The two coyotes that stood guard at her side stay. As I get closer I realize that they are grey wolves. Then I see that only one is a grey wolf, the other just a wolf. I follow the old woman into the trees. My memories of Dark-Eyes are with me and I wonder if he is close by, if my longing and emptiness will be over now.

I come into a camp. A tripod hangs over a fire, with soup cooking in it. A lean-to made of limbs and pine boughs nestles beside a cave where another fire flickers. The old woman sits beside the kettle and stirs. As I walk closer, I notice that her left hand is a wolf paw. I look into her face. She has one yellow eye and the face of a wolf. The other eye is an old woman's, gentle and soft and wrinkled. She looks up at me and says, "I am Grandmother Wolf."

She drops her head and her face becomes that of a two-legged. Her eyes are blacker than ebony and as the fire reflects in them, they're burgundy stars.

"Grandmother Burgundy Star?"

She looks at me and smiles. "I am. I am the teachings of Mother Nature. I am all that is absolute—all that will be correct. Sit with me. It's an ideal place to be. I will teach you of perfection. Things will become very clear and pure. You are in the presence of the teachings of burgundy—impeccability."

She stirs the soup. I keep thinking, "There's no place like home."

"Do you know what home is?" She looks at me with a stern darkness in her eyes. "Do you know what color black is when you aren't looking at it? Do you know the answer to a question?"

I recall the teachings that I have gathered from my visions. "The answer to the questions are what I believe is so. My belief is my answer," I reply.

She looks at me and says, "Very well. Confidence suits you. Balance is in your footsteps. Now what is your creativity, Granddaughter? Do you know what you are? Do you know which one you are? Do you know when you are? Do you know why and how? That is the answer to the question."

I'm in for a long teaching. At that moment there is a clap of thunder. A sparking fork of lightning bounces around the camp through the trees—there's a shimmering iridescent green all around me. I begin to feel fear. Then it dissipates and I have a sureness of what the green star is. I take a deep breath in and I remember the owl feather, the sacred spot of wisdom, and I let go. I—let—go. You can struggle and fight, put your shoulder behind it and only lose—nothing changes. I let go.

"Would you like some dinner, darling?" She smiles out of the side of her face.

" 'Darling' isn't a word that I like. It seems fake and over-used. It isn't me."

She says, "Do you know what the most precious thing you have is? Give me your most precious thing."

"I'm torn to choose the most precious thing to give away."

"Well, how will you answer the question?" she says.

The lessons flood my mind. There is an eeriness around me. Everywhere I look, beside every tree, inside the cave opening, along the stumps and everywhere, yellow eyes are peeking out at me.

"I believe my most precious thing would be what I am—Myself. That is my most precious thing."

She smiles, "Yourself is the answer. That is the most important thing you have. Yourself. And to be that, you must be whole."

She holds out four vegetables and says, "We'll build a soup and eat it. And when we do, the most precious thing you have will be complete."

The first vegetable is a whole potato. She says, "Our soup is the medicine of impeccability. It consists of absoluteness. We put a whole potato in it. The word 'whole' goes into the soup."

She pulls out a bunch of carrots. "The total here is four. Four begins with red as one, orange as two, yellow as three, and green as four." She cuts the carrots and throws the total of four into the soup. "Total is necessary."

She peels an onion and says, "It's clean, totally clean." She chops it and throws it into the soup and "clean" goes in.

She squashes a handful of tomatoes and puts them in. "This will make it full. I have put the absolute medicine into the soup. Whole. Total. Clean. Full.

"Now, choose between the next things. Do you wish fish or beef? Turtle meat, snake? Which is better?"

It is hard, but I choose the turtle. It seems so exotic. She throws it in. She looks at me and says, "Then you know what better is. How about fresh sea gull? It's quite a change."

"Hmm. I'm not sure."

She throws it in. I knew she would. She grins and it is a snarl. Ugh! Change.

"This is the call to account." We stir the soup in honor of the East, the South, the West and the North. "We add a tad of garlic to unmake, to take away the unwantedness, to release negativity. Now it's correct. Better, change, call to account, and unmake have been placed in the soup."

I am a little worried about the sea gull and the turtle. Ordinary is what I am used to.

"What is your goal? What is your aim? What is it that you choose to complete and be best at? Do you want to stay the same? These are ideal circumstances. Ideal medicine must go into the soup at this point, so I add herbs. State your goal."

She throws in some other ingredients. "These represent the aim." She stirs the soup. "Now taste it, and see if it's complete."

Mmmm. I am a little nervous, but I taste it. "Complete is a question."

"That's right. There will be soup that's the same and there will be soup that's better. But there won't be any best. There won't be any better than this. It is the best."

When she says "best," she lets the spoon of soup drip back into the pot. She says, "We've placed it in an ideal way now. Goals, aim, complete and best are in the soup. Now we'll look at it from a perfect angle. Is it good? Is it complete? Is it excellent? Is it unbounded?"

I say, "To make it good, I'd like some peas. To make it complete, I'd like some corn. It would be excellent if we removed the sea gull."

She dumps in the peas and the corn. "Excellent," she says, and throws in a couple more pieces of fresh sea gull. "Let go of the fear and it will be unbounded. Allow the flavors to mix. When this happens, perfect is at hand because it's just the way it is.

"Clarity comes to the soup now. Even and real, plain and certain." She places a rock in the soup and says, "It's even now." She takes the rock out and says, "It's real." She removes the sea gull and says, "Now it's plain." She asks me, "What is your most precious thing?"

I look her in the eye and say, "Myself."

She drops the sea gull back into the pot and says, "It is certain. The next medicine will be pure. Fair, perfect, genuine and sincere." She stirs and places the lid on the soup. "This is fair." It cooks for a while and she plays her flute.

"It must be perfect," I say.

"That's right," she says, "just the way it is."

It is her soup, and the teachings of impeccability that she wants me to hear. I wonder how she is going to reflect "genuine and sincere." In a while she takes the lid from the soup. She pours some into a bowl and hands it to me. "It's genuine now."

I taste it. Uhhh! It is different. Turtle and sea gull soup. She has thrown in a lot of other things, too. Roots, mushrooms, little funny-looking vegetables that I've never seen before. Perhaps she brings about impeccability, because she is sincere. My mind begins to figure it that way.

"What is your most precious thing?"

At that moment the air passage to my throat shuts off.

Grandmother steps up graciously, extending her hand, and there is the green star. "If you can tell me the ceremony of the seven black stars, you have grown. You have held your faith. You have a belief."

I feel empty. I breathe. Fear rushes inside of me, but I focus on what I know is so with my medicine.

"Grandmother Burgundy Star, the seven black stars lie ahead of me on the path of the mountains. I go back to the earth a two-legged, a different person, knowing the ways of the impeccable soup. To swallow perfect is just the way it is. Those are the hard times, aren't they, Grandmother? When things go wrong and you can't explain. When the old ones die and you move towards the light. That's the way, isn't it, Grandmother?"

She looks at me and lifts her lip. I see those large teeth but fear does not rush my body. I am in acceptance. I am steady as I look out over the vast canyon and mountains—beauty beyond words. If I could just step off into it forever!

"Out there you will go. You will quest for the whole self. Your adventure lies ahead of you." She whistles and the grey wolf comes to her side. "In this range of mountains the grey wolf is a native. It knows the way through Eagle Mountain. It follows the pass as the eagle flies—spirit moving across the land. It will give to you the best friend that you could have—the grey wolf—the one who will stand with you always. You quest for the whole self, to understand the two-legged walk. To bring that back and mark a way of obedience. To serve Great Spirit and honor Grandmother and Grandfather in a good way. To find the teachings of the seven black stars: this is your quest of the whole self."

"What is the whole self, Grandmother Burgundy Star? I know that I have learned from my vision and from the spirit keepers of the sacred stars that I am of wolf spirit. What is the whole self?"

When I ask this question of Grandmother Burgundy Star, she looks at me with one side of her face smiling and the other in a frown. At that moment an eagle flies around her and a mountain lion walks around her feet. Passing beside her is an elk, on her shoulder a raven. An owl stands on her arm. Running past her, circling us, throwing dirt high in the air, is a black-and-white horse. As its hooves strike the ground, sparks of burgundy fly. When the horse has circled seven times, it stops and begins to eat the grass.

"All of this is your wholeness. This is you—including me. I am you. Today you stand there. Tomorrow you stand here."

I look at her: beady eyes, small set. From one angle they are red, from another yellow; straight on they are dark burgundy. Her white hair is pulled back. She wears a burgundy jacket, and over it a cape-like smock. Her hands are withered but strong, teeth long and pointed, jaw strong and set.

"Look at yourself here. Now tell me who you are."

"I don't know, Grandmother. I have not my ways. I don't know the old medicine. I don't know individuality."

"Your vision has come for you, Little One. It has provided your path—the highest of all being the sun. You have walked to that circle where you have entered the gateways. There you have learned what sacred is. Now you come to the sacred teachings. What have you learned?"

"I have known fear, Grandmother. I have embraced it and seen my emptiness. I have found my loneliness is to be replaced only with the medicines that I have gained from each star. I have walked the shamanic path and there I have found Rainbow Medicine: Confidence from Grandfather Red Star, Balance from Grandfather Orange Star, Creativity from Grandfather Yellow Star. I have seen Growth from Grandmother Green Star, Truth from Grandmother Blue Star, and Wisdom from Grandmother Purple Star. I have come with you and dined on Impeccability. I feel that home is in this medicine."

She looks at me and I look at me. I look—at impeccability.

"This is your clan. This is your home—the seventh. Close your eyes and hold out your hand."

She places in my hand a wolf paw. "Hold this with you, always. In it is your medicine. You walk with the tale of the Wolf. It is yours to tell. You transform with Rainbow Medicine. It is yours to teach. Teaching allows the path that brings about growth. From there come changes. You transmute and from there you transform."

I look at the wolf's paw and it has changed to the green star. I hold my growth. Impeccability is perfect. It is like the soup, perfect just the way it is. I feel excitement growing inside me. I open my hand, and there is a burgundy star.

Grandmother laughs, the sun setting behind her. Evening has come. It is quiet on the path in the spirit world. Shades of the sunset reflect soft pale colors: red, orange, yellow, green, blue, purple, and burgundy. I look at the burgundy star again and I see the wolf's paw in my hand. My total self is mine to hold.

The wind comes up as evening falls. There's no place like home—the self.

I Hear the Rapid Beat of the Drum Calling Me Back.

Lodge Pole

The lodge pole is kept at your front door, just inside your home, where all will pass it when entering your space. Lean it in a corner or against the wall. It tells the story of you, so it should reflect all your medicine and your personality. It is a place to keep your feathers and medicine bundles, special objects and keepsakes.

Needed: *A long pole from 5–7 feet (1.5–2.1m); various objects from your life experiences*

The pole can be of any type of wood you choose. Find it by walking the beach or the woods, or removing it from a tree. Be sure to honor the wood with tobacco before removing it, and give thanks for the life of the wood.

When you place a colored cloth on the pole, make sure it is 100% cotton. Use cotton or wool string. When you hang objects on the lodge pole, tie them on with colored string or skin. We wrap the objects; it is also permissible to poke holes in the chosen objects, so that you can hang them on the lodge pole..

Preparing for the Teachings of Impeccability

Tools: *Cornmeal; tobacco; journal; drum or rattle; any other sacred tools; plus the objects listed below.*

The road to impeccability is narrow. It consists of hard work and, most of all, growth. Understand the realm of growth, and choices are yours.

1. **Find the objects.** Begin this process early in the day so that you will be finished in time to set up a ceremony at sunset.

The following objects may be found wherever you wish; for example, from your natural surroundings: shells, feathers, seeds, flowers, sticks, rocks. Or you can find within your belongings a special piece of cloth or clothing, sacred tools, a toy.

- First find four objects that represent the word "absolute": one for "whole," one for "total," one for "clean" and one for "full."

- Next find four objects for "correct": one for "better," one for "change," one for "calling to account," one for "unmake."

- Next find four objects that represent "ideal": one for "goal," one for "aim," one for "complete," one for "best."

- Next find four objects for "perfect": one for "good," one for "complete," one for "excellent," one for "unbounded."

- Then find four objects for "clarity": one for "even," one for "real," one for "plain," one for "certain."

- Finally find four objects for "pure": one for "fair," one for "perfect," one for "genuine" and one for "sincere."

2. **Find seven sticks** 14 inches (35cm) in length, diameter of your choice. You can make them from dowel rods, or you may find natural pieces of wood. If you find them in the woods, they are to be green—alive. Strip the bark, making the sticks peeled and smooth.

3. **Find seven pieces of cloth** 14 inches (35cm) long by an inch (2.5cm) wide in these colors: pink, peach, pale yellow, mint green, pale blue, lavender, and burgundy. Tie the pieces of cloth around the tops of the sticks so that seven inches (17.5cm) hang down on each side, making two seven-inch (17.5cm) ties. Using a knife or scissors, cut the two pieces, dividing them into two again, so that four streamers hang from the top of the stick.

4. **Find a sacred place** *wide open to the sky,* from which you can see the sunset—on a mountaintop, for example, at a high place in the desert, looking out at the ocean, or on a hillside in the country. You choose.

The Ceremony of Receiving the Teachings of Impeccability

Taking the objects you have found and the sticks with colored ties, go to the place that you have chosen to spend the evening.

1. **Prayer.** Take up your burgundy stick. Honor the Creator, the earth, your teachings and yourself by holding it over your heart. Place cornmeal on the ground to honor Earth Mother and all the earth spirits who will be there to help you. Place the stick in the ground and offer a prayer that you might know "absolute"; that "correct" will come for you; that "ideal situations" are there; that "perfect" is; that "clarity" is at hand; that "pure" is, and that all of this is "impeccability."

2. **Placing the objects.** Turn to the East and step out seven paces (one for each color) from the burgundy center stick. When you reach the seventh spot, put the pink stick in the ground. Then place the four objects, in their original order, moving towards the South.

   When you have placed the last object—representing "full," put the peach flag in the ground and then put its four accompanying objects on the ground. Continue this process, placing the pale yellow flag followed by four objects; the pale green flag and four objects; the pale blue flag and four objects; the pale purple flag and four objects. Space them so that you build a complete circle with your flags and your objects.

3. **Receiving symbols.** Now go to the center and take four breaths in and out. Using your drum or rattle to accompany you, prepare to receive a vision for "absolute." This vision will be an understanding of impeccability. Focus upon your objects of whole, total, clean and full, and receive a symbol for "absolute." Continue by focusing upon the orange objects and receive a symbol for "correct." Continue in the same way, receiving symbols for "ideal," "perfect," "clear" and "pure." Record these symbols in your journal.

4. **Listening to Great Spirit.** Sit with this ceremony until the sun is completely gone. Think about obtaining impeccability and understand what it will take to have this in your life. Listen to Great Spirit, and all that accompanies Great Spirit, to learn what these words will do for you, allowing you: to have a total life; to change and unmake anything that stands in the way of better; to find your aim and your goals and set your best in motion; to walk the good red road; to be

excellent and unbounded; to make things even; to accept and honor pain; to be certain and real; to know what fair is.

Accept that you are perfect just the way you are. Know that you will be genuine and sincere. Leave all unwanted stress in the circle.

5. **Finishing.** When you are finished with your feelings and the dark has come, gather your objects but leave the poles. Take up your objects and your bundle of other sacred tools and give thanks to the ground by leaving tobacco. Honor this site, so that you can always connect to it in your mind. Remember that you have made a connection with impeccability and that it is your walk to complete the cycle of the burgundy star.

Aho.

· 15 ·
The Moon

Before me I see a familiar path. I breathe in and out. I see poplar trees, with a full moon shining through. A soft evening breeze blows and the leaves shimmer. The moon calls me to walk in its light. As I walk, I am filled with my vision. I hold in my mind the teachings of the sun. Thank you, Father Sun, for the vision that you have given me, and the doors you allow me to walk through. Thank you, Grandmother and Grandfather Stars, for the lessons you have given me. Thank you for the guidance to know my path.

I look ahead and see a dog sitting with its head hanging. It does not talk, but conveys ideas through thought. It moves up the path. I hear no words, but it speaks to me to follow it.

"Come with me, quickly. I'll take you to the meeting of the moon, to the women who teach the cycle of flow. You'll understand about being a wolf, what Yellow Eyes has called you for."

I am intrigued by the old dog. He paces along at a good rate, a slight limp in his hip. I can tell he is a warrior of loyalty. I follow. The poplars become thicker and are joined by their cousins, the aspens. We move quickly through the fallen leaves on the ground, and the many tree people. I hear whispers of "Welcome," as we go through the thicket. I hear my heart beating. I listen to its drumbeat.

Ahead I see many women dancing and singing. They are all around me. The dog becomes one of them. I see a fire within the circle. I am drawn to four women. As I get closer, I recognize the dog person.

She says to me, "You have come to find the phase of the moon. To understand the teachings of Grandmother Moon in all the cycles that women are. In the center of this cycle, within the teachings, is the council of Mother Moon Elder. From Maiden Moon, to Mother, to Grandmother, to Great-Grandmother Old Hag. Here you will find the teachings of your clan, and where they draw their knowledge. We are glad that you have come."

"What is your name?" I ask respectfully.

She smiles. "I am known as Yellow Dog. I am the friend that is all a friend can be. Here, that is known as loyalty. It is a give-away.

"On earth, it is taken for granted. It is someone to do fun things with, someone who will be there. Someone who always is. Here you're going to be taught the lessons of loyalty. To understand that the way of the dog is the strongest commitment. Dependency does not exist in the spirit world. On earth it is a sad thing that people become dependent upon each other out of fear."

I listen to Yellow Dog, as I watch four moons dance within the circle—one moment women spinning, turning, leaping and dancing—the next, moons, circles of light around the fire.

"Within this circle is feminine energy. We all are females here. We're maidens, mothers, grandmothers, and great-grandmothers—the hags, the crones. We start off with energy that is small and go to the completeness of full."

I watch the spirits dance around the council fire. Every once in a while I get a glimpse of the moons within.

"You see the different phases of one," says Yellow Dog, friendly and unwelcoming at the same time. I feel comfortable with her, though, no uneasiness. She is full of joy and music—alive. "I'm going to take you to meet the moon."

As she moves towards the spirits who are dancing around the fire, they part, making a pathway. We walk close to the spirits, and at that moment all four in the center of the circle leap up above the fire. They hover together as one—one full moon, one side dark and one side light, a quarter on one side, its mirror on the other. Coming back to the ground, they dance around the fire again.

"I have a guest here for you," announces Yellow Dog.

The dancers circle me. They sit on the ground and motion for me to sit. Yellow Dog sits too. One of the dancers is soft, young and gentle and inviting. One is stronger, harder, older. One is even older, like water—deep. One is the oldest, you can tell—fear walks with this one.

They are transparent as I look at them, yet there.

"You sit here in the Council of the Moon to understand the beginning and end. Your vision starts with the youngest male energy and goes to the oldest female energy. You have gone from illuminate to abolish. Everything in between is your medicine," Yellow Dog says. "Now the teachings of the moon will come to you through the mothers of the moon."

The maiden begins to speak. Her eyes are red with yellow dots. Her hair is a shimmering brownish red, almost burgundy. When she stands, the fire in her form takes the shape of an eagle. She makes the shrill whistle of the eagle.

"I am the maiden, the waxing moon. Each month there are eleven days in my cycle. A time to think up ideas—'fresh' is the word. A time to start things—'new' is the word. A time when things get emotional—'clean' is the word. A time for foundation, for building—'bright' is the word. If you look beyond me, you will understand me as the thinker—a space where fresh, new, clean, and bright happens. Look into the air, for I am air. There you will see the guide, which represents the eastern section of your lodge."

I look beyond her into the still, rich and dark blue sky. There I see an eagle, circling, shrilling, soaring and floating.

"Hold that thought," the maiden says. "It is yours. It is the clan of the waxing moon for your vision." She quietly sits.

The next stands and says, "I am Mother. I am full moon. I have three days in the cycle of a month." She takes the form of a coyote. Her tale swishes as she speaks. I am looking into soft green eyes, soft hair, inviting features. As I look, her eyes become fire. "I am the one who carries through ideas. I make them happen. I am the doer. I get involved. I bring about the hardening. I make things complete. I have bondedness. I am unity. Look into the fire. There you will see your clan."

I gaze into her eyes and she disappears. There is the fire, the flames dancing. As I watch, a coyote darts here and there singing, looking. Other coyotes join. They are bonded. No lack of energy here, and much force. They share a meal, then they rest.

My mind returns to the four moons who sit with me. The next one speaks.

She says, "I am the waning moon—Grandmother." Her words flow like water. "I am busy. I recognize that I go from one thought to another. I work

Rainbow Medicine

on many ideas. I transform. I jump from one thing to another. I distort. I move one matter to another. I grow. I put a piece here and a piece there, together. I move around drastically. I have no boundaries. No rules. No limitations. Look at me, and you'll see your clan."

As I gaze at the Grandmother she is dark, yet light. She is quiet, yet noisy. Deep. Her eyes are forbearing. Within them I see a bear, reaching and grasping for food, yet lying still at the same time.

I blink, and again I sit in the circle. The fourth speaks.

"I am the wise old hag. The great-grandmother. I am the dark moon."

I feel an uneasiness, knowing that she is there, yet not. "I don't discuss. I argue with everything. I don't communicate new ideas. Cease is the word. I don't do anything and I can prevent others from doing anything. Overrule. I don't get involved and I don't care. Answer is the rule. Destroy, demolish, and clear away the old. Abolish is the rule. You know me well."

She looks at me, her eyes yellow, then red, then white. I see the earth covered with snow. Cold, dead, yet alive. Waiting to awaken. Standing in the snow is a wolf. It invites me with a look.

The circle of four is dancing around the fire. Yellow Dog says, "You have been blessed with the teachings of the four. The maiden represents the thinkers; the mother, doers; the grandmother, feelers; the hag, the council."

In the distance I see a woman dancing in free-flowing clothes of pale blue and white. Lifting her arms, spinning, she comes closer to me, closer and closer. She dances around me, her clothes floating in the wind. She stops and looks me in the eye. She is transparent. In her silver hair is a braid, and feathers are tied to it—two owl, two hawk, two eagle and two raven. In her face I see many things—the world, the water, the sky, a fire, the wind.

"What is your name?" I ask her.

Her look goes through me. I feel her name in my mind.

"My name is Moon Walker. And the four feathers on each side of my braid tell the story of my walk. I have come in your vision time to allow you to see your grandparents, to know the heart of your mother. To have the courage to be a grand teacher and to live what you have seen as your seven stars. You have heard the teachings of the moon and now you must become Wolf Moon Dance. Hold that name. The wolf is what you are—guide, teacher, warrior, protector, pathfinder, path leader. You have intensity and it is to be used in a burgundy way.

"I will give you now the test of knowing. I ask one simple question, 'What is your family that has walked before you?' Sit in sacred circle, draw from you mind the memory of spirit and bring it back to me."

I feel an absence. Emptiness is my opponent. I turn and there stands a scroungy old coyote. Dancing, it looks at me. It stands on its hind paws like a two-legged, swishing its tail, prancing around in its ratty old skin. It speaks. "You don't know the moon dance. You don't know your family. We've got you in a trap. We've caught you. You don't know the tale of the Wolf. You're empty of knowledge and tradition. All the visions in the world can never bring this back."

I hear a drum slowly beating in my heart. Softly, the wind blows in my mind. I see the moon with all her radiant beauty, the phases in front of me. I feel and I know.

Before me stands an aged native couple, dressed in the old way. Their love is strong as they hold hands. They have much wolf medicine with them, for they are mates for life. From them comes a child who stands with her mate. There is strength in their romance. From her comes a child who stands in her independence. Then her mate steps into the circle to be with her. They, too, stand with the energy of romance. From her I see myself. And then my half-side. We too stand in that circle.

Around us flies a strong and beautiful red hawk, with big wings and undersides of white and stripes. It lands on my shoulder—a familiar feeling. I watch myself standing with the hawk on my shoulder, and then it flies into the moonlight.

At my feet is a piece of wormwood. I place it in my medicine pouch. Before me I see the new moon. I hear words whispering through the wind, "Renew your hope. Understand that prayer and work bring freedom and truth."

Then the waxing crescent speaks, "New moon energy. Start now. Nurture and make things grow. Dare to dream."

I see the first quarter of the moon and hear the words "Focus. Focus now. Pull from me the self-confidence to renew. Go down the river easy. Let go."

Full moon speaks. "A time of wishes and dreams lies ahead—all your desires and the totality of your vision. Be thankful. Walk into the ceremony of celebration. But remember what is behind you."

The vision fades. I am looking at a dark sky. Moon Walker reminds me of the piece of wormwood I have placed in my medicine pouch. "Take the wood into your hand," she says.

"The medicine it holds is bitter medicine. It's the dark, the absence, the grief of non-acceptance that is deeper than the ocean. To be turned away. The dark side. You must remember the bitterness to understand the sweet. Do you see this?" she asks.

I take a deep breath and nod. "I understand. When something is lost, something is gained. And when something is gained, something is lost. It's too late when it's over. The bitter and the sweet. It brings about balance."

I turn to Moon Walker but all that is there is dark sky. Then before me I see the waning quarter. A stern but soft voice says, "Cry and plead for help. Understand that to help others is to help yourself. This waning time is a time to give, to help and to put yourself in touch with your needs. Know your needs and wants. This quarter I am soft, a time of healing dreams. Step into dream time. Look within and tap the power, the power that is your individuality. Draw from it and create."

Next I see the waning crescent. I have a sense of foreboding, mysterious and hidden. A small laughter comes, "I am a time of hidden secrets becoming known. My medicine is seeing and remembering all, looking within and understanding."

Then the dark moon. Nothingness, yet the moon. "Remember the ancient wisdom of now you see it, now you don't. When you don't see it, where is it? Gone, we like to think. But no, it is in its depth."

I wake as the sun comes up alongside the river. I lie in my medicine blanket, a blanket I hold dear to my heart, and look at the river in the morning light, remembering the words of the moon and the beautiful couples that are my family. All the directions are there—the knowledge of the earth, the sky and the sun.

The seven stars—the teachings. I keep hearing the words, "the teachings," as I fold my medicine blanket. My blanket is blue with stripes of color, bordered by a burgundy rim. The truth that I have gathered from my vision is the main medicine of this blanket and it is bordered in impeccability.

I put my bundle together to start my walk of my day. I go to the spirit world where the great teachers are. I hold the visions in my heart, and I know that from them I gain the strength of the teachings of the seven stars, Rainbow Medicine. I pass through the gateways in the medicine wheel that allow me to be in the face of the sun. The moon holds me and teaches as a grandmother. This is my family: the sun and the moon and the seven stars.

I Hear the Rapid Beat of the Drum Calling Me Back.

Snake Bundle

The snake bundle is used any time you want to move away from something.

Needed: *Silver cloth 16 inches (40cm) square; special objects that represent nurture, growth and change—feathers, stones, animal fur or skin*

The bundle is built by placing the silver cloth down flat with the corner points at top and bottom, left and right. Set your intention of change and growth by thinking about and working with your topic.

> *Example:* Stop smoking. Sit with the silver cloth and feel the energy of the snake, the one who sheds his skin and moves on. See the act of smoking, the years of hurting your health, the wasted money. Look at the cloth and see yourself moving away from smoking—see yourself NOT smoking. Then place a piece of amethyst rock in the cloth to help you remember NOT to smoke. Place fresh tobacco to honor the passing on of smoking to the sacred ceremony of tobacco as a prayer tool. Place other objects such as fresh rose petals to represent the beauty of your health and other things that have meaning for you.

Then say a prayer and close the bundle by placing the right corner over the center (which represents the East), then the left corner over the center, then pull the bottom corner up over the center and roll towards the top. Tie with a string.

The Snake Bundle is to be carried on your person by placing it in a medicine pouch or in your pocket. When you are working on change or transformation and complete the change work, place the bundle on your lodge pole. You may use the bundle any time. Just sit with it and put new intention in it by placing thought in the bundle.

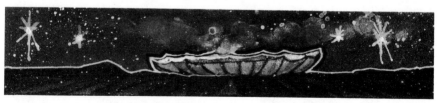

The Ceremony of the Moon

Tools: *Journal and pen; any sacred objects*

1. **Defining wants and needs.** Sit in a sacred circle (see page 43) and write the words "family," "brother," "sister," "mother," "father,"

"grandmother," "grandfather," "great-grandmother," "great-grand-father," "uncle," "aunt," "cousin," "niece," "nephew." Sit with each one of these words and define the needs and wants of each one. Make sure you understand the difference between "need" and "want." Understand their expectations and their limitations. Find what is yours, and what is theirs.

Now write the words "friend," "lover," "husband" or "wife," or any of the other relationships that concern you.

2. **The seven questions.** Ask yourself the following questions:

1. Where is the confidence within each of these words?
   Example: Sister. To have a sister gives me a feeling I am not alone. "Not alone" is Confidence.
2. Where is the balance?
   Example: To have a sister is to know what family is. This is Balance. To be able to know what a sister is and to know what it would be like without one is Balance.
3. Where is the creativity?
   Example: "Gives me a feeling" is Creativity. To construct a feeling is Creating.
4. Where is the growth?
   Example: Being able to feel and know is the ongoing process of growth.
5. Where is the truth?
   Example: To have a sister is a truth.
6. Where is the wisdom?
   Example: To see and understand the truth of a sister is wisdom.
7. Where is the impeccability?
   Example: The wholeness of all this feeling is impeccability—to feel and know, to have and to be.

After you have answered all these questions for each of these words, sit with your answers for a moment. Ask yourself what are you needs and what are your wants from each of these words.

3. Wait till the dark of the night, then **sit with whatever energy of the moon is there** that night. Breathe in and out four times. Look at the moon, receive a symbol for each one of the words and record it in your journal.

   Example: Brother. I look at the moon and see a wolf leaping over a fence. I interpret this as meaning that my path is never closed. There are no limits to the path of the experience of a brother.

Brother is the guide that takes you outside of your boundaries.

Interpret each symbol for each of your family members and for the words of love that are necessary to understand the depth of relationship with others. With this sacred ceremony, you connect to the mother energy—to the one who asks you to walk the path in your wholeness.

Aho.

· 16 ·

The Sacred Quest for the Whole Self

Before me I see a familiar path. I breathe in and out. The path takes me along a gravel road, and down to the river where I walk with a broken heart. I feel sadness and a need for acceptance. In my hand I hold a blue heart of many facets that I have taken from my medicine pouch. In my other hand I hold a burgundy heart. They are carved from stone and light passes through the blue one. The burgundy heart looks black, until you see it in the light.

I hold these hearts together in my hands and remember the sacred twins, the North and South, the East and West. Twins exist in lesson form, to show you the dark side of yourself, to show you what torn apart truly is.

The mind is one, then two, then four, then seven. "You are called to teach that, Wolf," says Burgundy Heart. "It is your job to lay the path. Grandmother Wolf wishes to speak to you. You must come to the mountains. It is time to start the initiation of the seven black stars."

"It's a long way to where Grandmother Wolf lives," I reply. I look down the river and there stands a gorgeous black horse of enormous power. "I will carry you to Grandmother Wolf," he says. "Hop on my back and we'll ride. Come now. Grandmother wishes to speak."

I mount the black horse and her swiftness cuts through the day and into the night until we finally arrive in the forest where Grandmother lives.

There stands the old grandmother, the wolf woman. "Life's answers are hard—filled with pain," she says. "This stops the two-legged. Answers are cried for and teachings are needed. That's all there is in this school, you know. Take one pain and one problem and replace it with one knowledge and one gain. Wolf, you must teach. There are those who seek the way. There are those who wish to know their way home—to find joy, to walk with discipline, to reach for the stars and heal the scars.

"These stars have doorways that you must enter. Find the answers and give them away. This is your walk as a two-legged.

"There are four levels, Wolf. The seven black stars become colored. Within each of these colored stars is a quarter of the sacred quest for the whole self. You see, two-leggeds search for the answer "Why," but there is more than that: a way of achieving is what lies ahead. The ability to take the blackness of abuse and make it what it is, a deeper shade of burgundy. When light is seen through black, you see what it is, a deeper shade of burgundy. It is for you to walk with the teachings of Rainbow Medicine. To bring forth your interpretation of the word sacred and to give to those who seek a way to find their wholeness. I want you to come with me now, and step out on the black stars."

The old wolf starts to work her way along a path that leads high into the mountains. I follow her. We come across a very narrow stretch along the mountain's edge, at the summit. It is a long way to fall.

"Now, we'll step into the sky onto the first black star and walk our way to the seventh, where we will reveal the sacred quest for the whole self."

The wolf steps into the sky and stands on a black star. "Come," she says. "Where is your confidence?" I step from the ridge of the mountain, out onto the black star. Standing in the sky is like nothing I have ever felt, secure yet insecure. She steps again. "Next one, Wolf. Your balance." I step out again. As I do, I recall all my earthly pain. I remember feeling inadequate, not good enough, being measured against someone else, pitted against someone's desire. But I stand on the black star. "Your balance you have," she says.

She jumps to the next one. Her leap is fierce and beautiful. "Your creativity—make it like you want it." I step across with grace and as I do, I think, "I can do, have and be all that I am."

She steps again, but slips and hangs on by a point. She comes up from the other side, by walking beneath the star. No words are spoken, as she motions me forward. I freeze, looking at the fourth star. I think of the green, and how obtainable it looks when it is black. How hard it was to find when I searched for it. "You cannot hold on to growth. You must simply leap." And I do. The leap of faith between the yellow and green.

I stand on the green star. Right in the middle. YES! With my hand clenched in a fist. YES! My vision is true. I have no fear of the leap of faith.

As she goes to the next black star—so do I, and we stand on the blue, in our hearts. Then I am standing on the fifth black star and she leaps to the next one. So do I. We stand on the sixth and I look at her beside me.

To the seventh one, she does not go. Only I. Standing on the seventh star, my heart pounding, I hear the drum. A shrill whistle calls and above me soars a grand eagle. It drops a spotted feather at my feet. I pick it up and see that it is finished in burgundy beads. On the end is a piece of fluff.

Grandmother says, as she stands on the sixth star, "You're home. You have been called to walk with the teachings of spirit. Some call it 'person of the cloth,' or a holy person, or shaman. Others don't know what to call it. What do you call it, Wolf? What is it for you?" I look at her and the six black stars. I turn and look into the vastness. There is a soft pastel light ahead of me, with bold red, orange, yellow, green, blue, purple and burgundy stripes.

"What do I call it? I call it a vision, Grandmother. I've had a vision. I see before me a bridge. A rainbow bridge that allows me to dance. I call it being a teacher, Grandmother. One who has the answers to her own questions. The grand teachings of the Sacred Red Road. I know the other side. I see it clearly ahead of me, across the bridge that I walk.

"I want to cross that bridge now, Grandmother. I want to see what's on the other side. I want to teach what I hear in my heart to those who want to know. I feel that I shouldn't jump, but I should."

"Don't jump too soon, and don't stay too long," she smiles.

"I've seen the treacherous ways of humans. As I go from the spirit world to be a two-legged I carry with me these colors as my family. I know my father as the red, orange and yellow; my mother as the green, blue, purple and burgundy.

"Grandmother, it is the sacred quest of the whole self that I hold inside my vision. I know this."

"This is so, Wolf. Remember the word, know your ancestors and hold within you the teachings of burgundy. Stand proud in what you achieve and what you build. You must have wholeness—totality—the ability to be black and white, to know black and white."

The Sacred Quest for the Whole Self   177

"Grandmother, Dark-Eyes has said that there is no such thing as black and white, only grey."

"Dark-Eyes tests your confidence! You know what black and white is. Speak to me, Granddaughter. Let us hear your words."

"White is the sacred spiritual walk. White is the spirituality that we seek on our earth walk, and white is the spirituality of our eternal existence. All color and spirit is what I know white to be. The sacred keepers of white must honor it always.

"Black is the blend of all that is material, in a physical way. Things that come to be, and all things that have been—poured together and bringing forth the truth of impeccability. Black is absolute. It is clarity and pureness. It holds within it the lessons of nothing, the questions of evil, the push and pull of 'bad.' It has the integrity of introspection."

I look at Grandmother for her approval, but she is gone. All that I see are the six black stars and on each of them a burgundy wolf's pawprint. I feel sadness for a moment. I turn to the bridge and I cross over.

I stand in nowness, right here. I breathe in and out. I'm walking along the ocean. Sea grass is all around me, waving in the night wind. The moon is bright and full. I carry with me as a two-legged a lot of pain and a sadness comes over me. I look at different things in my life and I see doors shutting. Rejection haunts me—I'm not good enough. I look at those places where not good enough is my very knowing. I look out to the ocean. As the waves roll over one another, I feel drawn to walk into them, to give up and close the door myself. I shake my head and breathe.

This is not so in the spirit world. This is not so on this path.

I begin gathering wood and I dig a small sand pit by the ocean, where I build a roaring fire. I notice the moon glistening on each piece of wood as I feed it into the fire. And then I realize that the wood is bones. It seems to be pieces of the things and people who have hurt me. I feel unbalanced. I choose not to do this. I wish not to destroy or hurt others as I have been hurt. There is no balance in that, no reconciliation.

A sea gull circles overhead in the moonlight. The sounds of the ocean comfort me and I look to Grandmother Moon for guidance. I sit with the fire and watch the sparks dance in the sky. I recall the moons as they danced over the flame and taught me lessons.

I want so much to have Grandmother Wolf' approval. I peer out at the ocean and watch the waves tumble in. Up the beach I see a small fire. I feel the presence of a wise one there, and I start to walk. I come to a camp with a beach house built of driftwood. Beside it I see pawprints of a wolf in the sand. I need to know who is here. Medicine is hanging on the walls of the driftwood house. Teachings are around me.

I step into the cabin and, as I do, I feel welcome but not. I sense someone is watching me. I go back out to the fire, which is soft and gentle.

"Hello? Is anyone around?"

Along the shoreline I see a wolf moving in a fast lope. As it circles towards me, I see that it is a grey wolf. It comes closer and becomes a woman. Her eyes are blue as the sky. There is a roughness like a sailor, someone who is tattered and worn by her passing days. She spits to the ground.

"Why are you in my home? Have I something that is yours?"

I look at her eyes and beyond the blue human eyes I see yellow eyes: the wolf is evident in her soul.

"Why have you come here?" I ask her.

"I live here. What's your excuse?" she replies.

"It's a funny thing to find you here along the shore. I see no two-legged marks. Only wolves."

"Mind your own business," she answers.

We both look out at the ocean.

"Well, what brings you here?"

"Oh, I come to forget Dark-Eyes. I come to let go of clichés, glitches, snags, illusions and disillusions. I'm walking my vision," I reply.

Her eyes cut to me. She says, "I'm interested. I see something in your face that is familiar. What is that object that you hold in your hands?"

"This?" I raise my hand. In it I have my prayer stick. "This is one with many colors. This is Willie, my prayer stick. I sit with Willie and connect. I've been called to teach the power within this stick, to follow the Rainbow Path and lead the way for those who look for their wholeness. I carry the Seven Sacred Teachings of the Rainbow Path. I have come here to the spirit world to relax and listen to Grandfather and Grandmother. Now I meet another who seeks the Path. I see this in your eyes."

We go inside the little cabin, build a fire, drink coffee, and talk of the miseries of being a two-legged—the pains and disconnections, the wrong moves and stupidities.

I say, "The lessons of the sacred teachings are dear to my heart. Let me show you the way home."

I Hear the Rapid Beat of the Drum Calling Me Back.

The Prayer Stick

The stick is used to center, to draw power, to fill a need of connection to the earth, sky, air and water. The stick will give a setting of sacred space, where your prayer work can proceed.

Needed: *Stick 12–14 inches (30–35cm) long, of cottonwood, aspen, birch or pine; a strip of red 100% cotton cloth ¼ inch (.6cm) long; seashells; moss; stones and feathers; various colors of 100% cotton or wool string or yarn*

The prayer stick is made by winding colored threads around the stick. Think of the medicine for each color as you wind it.

A special stone—such as one given to you by family or friend, one you've found on a walk, or a gemstone—is tied to the top of the stick to give grounding power, because you need to be focused on your prayers.

Tie feathers or other animal medicine on the stick to guide you through the subject you are praying about. When the stick is all dressed up, sit with the stick to give you balance and truth.

The Ceremony to Hear the Calling of Your Wholeness

Tools: *7 candles: red, orange, yellow, green, blue, purple and burgundy; journal and pen; sacred objects*

To quest for is to seek. The Sacred Quest for the Whole Self is a ceremony. It takes you deep within yourself and allows you to experience your confidence, your balance, your creativity, your growth, your truth, your wisdom and your impeccability. The following ceremony is to hear the calling of your wholeness. There are four steps:

1. **Awareness.** On the night of a full moon, sit with the seven colored candles and build a circle of flame in front of you. In your journal list all the things that you long for, the needs that you have as an individual. Then list the things that keep you from having them, the things that get in the way. Sit with this list and study what you have brought forth. Become aware of your wholeness, of your needs, and evaluate the things that get in your way.

   Example: My needs are my vision and the steps that it holds within it, such as writing, lecturing and teaching. The things that get in my way are a lack of organization, a lack of vision, a lack of sincerity.

2. **Openness.** To achieve openness, journal the things that you deny. Sit with yourself and pull these denials out. Identify the places in which you feel your energy leaving you. Most important, if you say you have no denials, then start there.

   Example: Weakness. Lack of confidence. Lack of concern. Fear. Intense anger.

3. **Call for a teacher.** Sit with your ring of colors and take four deep breaths. Before you, you'll see a white, very intense light. Out of that light will come symbols, possibly trees or stones, plants or animals. It will give you the clues that you need in order to establish a personal relationship with a teacher.

4. **Listen.** Now sit with your candles and listen to yourself. Listen for your acceptance, your appreciation, your needs, your weaknesses, your strengths. Listen for your will to live and for the mystery of life. Record what you hear and see.

From this ceremony you may draw an understanding of the calling of your wholeness. Doors will open for you to study the areas in your life that keep you from your wholeness. When you feel the warmth of the sun and the cool of the moon, it is time to dance with the stars. With Rainbow Medicine, you feel and live the heartbeat of your life.

Aho.

Medicine Interpretations

The following interpretations may help you understand your visions and the depth of your walk as a two-legged on the earth.

The Colors

P. 178
Black & white

Red—Confidence, Strength, Nurture, Absolute, Illumination, Beginning, Accountability

Orange—Balance, Success, Choice, Correct, Following, Preceding, Responsibility

Yellow—Creativity, Vision, Ceremony, Ideal, Solidity, Sincerity

Green—Growth, Beauty, Change, Perfect, Faith, Innocence, Honest

Blue—Truth, Healing, Proof, Clarity, Introspection, Depth, Faithful, Understanding

Purple—Wisdom, Power, Real, Pure, Commitment

Burgundy—Impeccable, Great, Grand, Mystery, The Path

Animal Spirit Helpers—The Four-Legged

Bat—Has the ability to distinguish between things and to apply action at the right moment. To bring to rebirth.

Bear—Teaches us to go within. Asks us to look at our lives, at all aspects and all costs, to find the truth that lies within. To look at things in an adult way and be mature about our decisions. To understand that individual thoughts come from within.

Beaver—Allows us to dream, helps us to build those dreams. Building, making happen, taking a new path.

Coyote—Two-sided. To walk in a way that will help us to balance and to receive the life-bearing force. Coyote tells us of the need to pay attention. It may be understood as growth.

Crow—Asks us to be organized and sets things in a way that is balanced. Asks us not to fall short of what is so for ourselves. To keep in touch with what we long for. Not to give up. If we do, it is death.

Deer—Teaches us to pay attention to our emotions. To understand the swing between physical and spiritual. Not to run quicker than we're able. Not to leave too soon, not to stay too long. The emotional swing, as well as the gentle emotional steady.

Dog—Opens doors to loyalty. To have the ability to understand "conditional." To realize the "unconditional" is a condition. To see the loop. To understand the "go around, come around." Every little dog has its day.

Eagle—Connection with Great Spirit. When you see the eagle in your vision, it is a connection to the Seven Sacred Teachings and brings an understanding of totality. There can be nothing missing when the eagle is at hand. The need for the greatest respect and honoring is necessary. To understand that Great Spirit is listening and approving of your ways.

Fox—Gives us the ability to know, to have the wit and the cleverness, as well as the willingness to hang in there.

Frog—Brings clarity, the ability to clean away the clutter and the unwanted, and to bring forth what is so for you.

Hawk—Listening. The ability to hear the message of Great Spirit. To have and interpret visions and dreams.

Horse—Self-empowerment. The ability to look to the thunder beings and the lightning beings, to walk with thunderbird medicine. To take the teachings of the clans, the Seven Sacred Teachings, and have the power to understand medicine. To walk the medicine path in a physical way.

Lizard—Has to do with change, the movement from one station to another and becoming as that station is. Marks the movement of dreams. Are they real? Are they an illusion? It is the ability to know what is real.

Mouse—Does the work of pick, pick, pick, and being prepared. Mouse analyzes and organizes, working to bring forth. It helps us realize that we are very small in Grandfather's plan, yet very powerful.

Raven—The sacred keeper of magic, the one who guards the spiritual teachings. The magical power. The ability to look beyond, remember Grandfather's color and bring it into reality. The raven stands as guard of the void.

Skunk—Genuine. The ability to take things at their greatest and to accept. Not to worry about what others think, but to know that you have the power to stand your own ground.

Snake—The act of transformation, of medicine. To be able to shed your skin and leave your shadow as a ghost. To look back, comprehend the memory and use it as a lesson.

Squirrel—Intelligence. Knowing that the cycle has a beginning, middle and an end. The squirrel is prepared to store up for a rainy day, to be connected and to understand that there is a tomorrow to be prepared for.

Wolf—The symbol of the teacher, pathfinder, protector, warrior. One who knows. The shaman, the transformer, the healer, the sorcerer. The parent.

Insect and Other Spirit Helpers—The Crawlies

Ant—Patience, hard work, togetherness, order, rules.

Butterfly—Beauty, faith, change, sacredness. Also, the circle, opening, the beginning and end, transformation.

Beetle—Innocence, movement, purpose.

Centipede (thousand-legged)—Awareness, sincerity. To touch.

Cockroach—Eternal, long-lasting. Reproduction.

Dragonfly—Dreamtime, illusion, vision. Knowing. A doorway.

Lady Bug—Luck, fortune, money, work, planning.

Potato Bug (or Roly Poly)—Play, protection, childhood.

Scorpion—Strength, intensity, depth. Intelligence. Survival.

Slug—Keeping on. No limits. Smooth, unconditional, slow.

Snail—Home, warmth, comfort.

Spider—Learning, teaching, hearing. A storyteller, trickster.

Tree Spirit Helpers—The Standing People

The tree people have many stories to tell us. Trees hold within stability and strength, sincerity, peace, and the recall of ancient wisdom.

Alder—The ability to know oneself. Balance and acceptance of the self. Seeing the good and the bad, finding integrity, harmony, peace.

Apple—Passion, sexual and otherwise, romance and the renewal of romance. The act of love. The love medicine tree.

Ash—Truth, sincerity, compassion and understanding.

Aspen—Knowing, intuition, discernment, forgiveness.

Birch—Quiet, tolerant, the ability to see, to listen, to think. Realization.

Cedar—Cleansing, release, purification, renewal and replacement.

Cherry—The ability to produce, productivity, success, achievement.

Dogwood—Spiritual inspiration. The ability to see harmony, to distinguish between.

Eucalyptus—Transformation, transmutation, nurturing, kindness.

Fir—Ancient wisdom. The depth of purification. Restoring and regeneration.

Fire maple—Intense energy. Lifting from a lull to a high-pitch.

Fruit—The medicine of bringing forth—to create, to bear. Contain the medicine wheel teachings of the full cycle from seed to tree to fruit to seed. Abundance and prosperity.

Hemlock—Vanishing, doing away with, cleansing, renewal, cycling.

Maple—Luck and strength.

Oak—Steadfastness, stability, power, might and protection. Carrying an acorn with you will bring protection.

Pear—Hope, faith, growth, generosity.

Pine—Ancient wisdom, impeccability, eternal life.

Poplar—Vision, peace, achievement.

Redwood—Strength, longevity, memory and maturity.

Walnut—Confidence and energy.

Willow—Mystic visions. Being open to clairvoyance. The powers of the third eye. Friendship, luck, bending, continuing, going with the flow.

The Plant Spirit Helpers—The Rooted People

Angelica—Helps with anxiety, weakness, nervous stomach, hopelessness. Balancing.

Balm—Protection, melancholy, anger, rage, and sadness. Soothes sleeplessness and restless sleep.

Bergamot—Nervous tension, stress. Encouraging.

Cedar—Fear, anger, psychological disconnection. Calming, warming, honoring, harmony and comfort.

Chamomile—Tension, over-sensitivity. Used during pregnancy, calming, receiving.

Cypress—Collecting one's thoughts. Weak-minded, forgetful. Sexual craving. Sobbing. Aids resting, calming. Sedative. Gentle atmosphere.

Eucalyptus—Emotional overload, struggling. Balance, stimulation, focus.

Geranium—Harmony and comfort.

Grapefruit—Harmony and comfort.

Honey Clover—Aids resting, calming. Sedative. Gentle atmosphere.

Hyssop—Clarity, concentration, cleansing, creativity, meditation, centering, extreme mood shifting, emotions. Aids with work area and working. Produces stimulation, increases concentration. Refreshes and slows down fatigue.

Jasmine—Low self-esteem, weakness, emotions, suffering, and fear. Confidence.

Juniper Lime—Aids with work area and working. Produces stimulation, increases concentration. Refreshes and slows down fatigue.

Lavender—Strengthening, refreshing, clairvoyance, mood swings. Divination. Headaches, insect bites. Harmony and comfort. Aids resting, calming. Sedative. Gentle atmosphere.

Lime—Aids with work area and working. Produces stimulation, increases concentration. Refreshes and slows down fatigue.

Mint—Memory, loss of memory, unclear thinking, shock. Aids with work area and working. Produces stimulation, increases concentration. Refreshes and slows down fatigue.

Orange—Sensuality, self-consciousness, selfishness. Balancing and relaxing. Harmony and comfort.

Patchouli—Protection, attraction, sexual awareness.

Roman Chamomile—Aids resting, calming. Sedative. Gentle atmosphere.

Rose—Strengthening the inner being. Disappointment, sadness. Aids resting, calming. Sedative. Gentle atmosphere.

Rosemary—Uplifting the ego, empathy, poor memory.

Sage—Sacred honor, opening, cleansing, protection.

Sandalwood—Harmony, stress, nervous tension.

Swiss Pine—Aids with work area and working. Produces stimulation, increases concentration. Refreshes and slows down fatigue.

Tangerine—Harmony and comfort.

Yarrow—Menopause, marriage, confusion, open awareness. Energies.

Rock Spirit Helpers—The Solid Ones

It's good to build a medicine pouch so that you can carry the rock people around with you. Or wear a stone set in a ring to connect you with the medicine of the rock people.

Agate—Courage, luck and prosperity. Appreciation of nature.

Amber—Romantic love, patience, memory.

Amethyst—Modification. Modifying eating habits, drinking, use of drugs. Promotes awareness, meditation, balance, psychic ability and understanding of death. Gives us the wisdom to ask for our new life that lies ahead of us. Wisdom is a key point.

Crystals—Clarity of thought, memory, communication, awakening, visualization. They amplify prayers and wishes.

Diamond—Bonds. Gives courage and purity, longevity. Helps us find things.

Double-Terminated Crystal—Allows energy to cycle. Allows us to recall dreams and have psychic ability. It also eases access to the spirit world.

Gold—Brings about wealth. An attracting energy, giving positive thoughts. Allows opportunity and courage.

Moonstone—Safe travel on water. Hope and new beginnings.

Obsidian—Protection, introspection, fulfillment, inner growth. Helps us get in touch with our feelings.

Ruby (a raw ruby)—Spiritual protection.

Silver—Visions, hope and grounding.

Tiger's Eye—Clear thinking, courage and willpower. Empowerment.

Turquoise—Empathy, general healing, transformation, transmutation, renewal, release, emotional sensitivity. Appreciation of nature.

Index